D1009290

Titles in the series

www.amazingstoriesbooks.com

LATE-BREAKING
AMAZING STORIES™

CRYSTAL METH

The #1 drug problem in North America

by Nate Hendley

Altitude Publishing

PUBLISHED BY ALTITUDE PUBLISHING LTD.
1500 Railway Avenue, Canmore, Alberta T1W 1P6
www.amazingstoriesbooks.com
1-800-957-6888

Extreme care has been taken to ensure that the information contained
in this book is accurate and up to date at the time of printing. However,
neither the author nor the publisher is responsible for errors, omissions,
loss of income or anything else that may result from the information
contained in this book.

All web site URLs mentioned in this book were correct at the time of
printing. The publisher is not responsible for the content of external
web sites or changes which may have occurred since publication.

In order to make this book as universal as possible, all currency
is shown in U.S. dollars.

Publisher	Stephen Hutchings
Associate Publisher	Kara Turner
Canadian Editors	Melanie Jones and Frances Purslow
U.S. Editor	Julian S. Martin
Charts	Scott Dutton

We acknowledge the financial support of the Government
of Canada through the Book Publishing Industry Development
Program (BPIDP) for our publishing activities.

ALTITUDE GREENTREE PROGRAM
Altitude Publishing will plant twice as many trees as were used
in the manufacturing of this product.

Cataloging in Publication Data
Hendley, Nate
    Crystal meth / Nate Hendley.

(Late-breaking amazing stories)
ISBN 1-55265-307-2 (American mass market edition)
ISBN 1-55439-508-9 (Canadian mass market edition)

    1. Methamphetamine abuse--United States. I. Title. II. Series.

HV5825.H45 2005a	362.29'9	C2005-905777-7 (U.S.)
HV5825.H45 2005	362.29'9	C2005-905768-8 (Cdn)

In Canada, Amazing Stories® is a registered trademark of Altitude Publishing
Canada Ltd. An application for the same trademark is pending in the U.S.

Printed and bound in Canada by Friesens
2 4 6 8 9 7 5 3 1

This book is dedicated to the
wild and wonderful Fischer sisters,
Alyson, Erin, and Anne-Marie.

CONTENTS

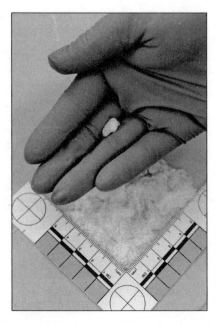

An Oklahoma State Bureau of Investigation employee
poses with 6.4 grams of crystal methamphetamine
seized in a drug bust, in Oklahoma City, in August
2005. Oklahoma's meth lab seizures have fallen
90 percent since it became the first state to ban
over-the-counter sales of cold medicine.

Fresno Meth Task Force investigators examine the charred ruins of a Meth "super lab" that exploded in flames near Madera, California in 2003. The meth lab reignited when Meth Task Force members later tried to remove some combustible red phosphorus. For more on the dangers of meth labs, see page 55.

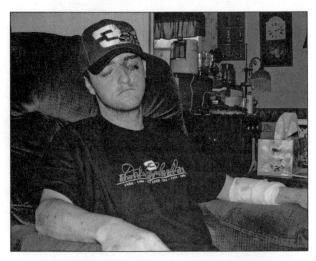

Former meth user Michael Murphy sits in his parent's rural St. Clair, Missouri, home in February 2005, reflecting on the day a tank of anhydrous ammonia blew up in his face. The accident left him blind in both eyes, deaf in one ear, and with chemical burns and shrapnel wounds on his body.

Tennessee Govenor Phil Bredesen announces the
statewide methamphetamine education campaign
"Meth Destroys" at Merrol Hyde Magnet School in
Hendersonville, Tennessee, November 7, 2005. The
campaign carries a proactive message to young people
and their communities about the dangers of the drug.

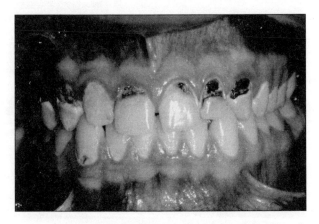

This photograph, provided courtesy of the University of
Kentucky College of Dentistry, shows the teeth
of a methamphetamine user. A condition called
"meth mouth" results from the drug's tendency
to dry out saliva, which defends teeth against rotting.
For more information about the drug's
side effects, see page 31.

Florida Department of Law Enforcement special agent supervisor Ed Hudson stands behind some of the common household products that typically are used in clandestine laboratories to make methamphetamine. See Chapter 2 for more information about the drug's chemisty.

CHAPTER 1

Introducing Meth

On February 21, 2003, David Parnell—a sometime factory worker and full-time methamphetamine addict—tried to kill himself with an SKS assault rifle. The 36-year-old had taken to toting the weapon around his Martin, Tennessee, home, shooting at bushes, trees, and other objects that triggered his raging paranoia. In his high strung, sleep-deprived state, menace lurked behind every blade of grass and bit of flora.

Parnell's body was as wired as his mind. By this point, his weight was down to 160 pounds, from a high of 200. Muscular and handsome in a rough-cut fashion, Parnell was showing signs of extreme stress and hard living. His temper was explosive, he babbled to himself at high speed, and he heard voices in his head. Co-workers at the tire plant in Mayfield, Kentucky, where Parnell was nominally employed, were becoming nervous.

Parnell's main drug of choice was methamphetamine (meth), an illegal and super-potent brand of the stimulant amphetamine. Meth isn't something that's smuggled in from Colombia or Asia's golden triangle. An entirely synthetic drug, meth is made in makeshift labs in motels, trailers and other locales across North America. A white, odorless powder, methamphetamine dissolves easily in water. The drug can also come in white or yellow chunks that resemble rock salt.

Also called crank, speed, and crystal—among other names—meth spent decades

STREET TERMS FOR METHAMPHETAMINE		
Biker's coffee	Granulated orange	Sketch
Blue meth	Hot ice	Speed
Chalk	Ice	Spoosh
Chicken feed	Kaksonjae	Stove top
Cinnamon	L.A. glass	Super ice
Crank	Lemon drop	Tick tick
Crink	Meth	Trash
Crystal meth	Methlies quick	Wash
Desocsins	OZs	Working man's cocaine
Geep	Peanut butter	Yellow barn
Glass	Shabu	Yellow powder

in obscurity, known only to bikers and blue-collar workers. In the past few years, however, it's achieved mass popularity.

Parnell took methamphetamine for a variety of reasons. Meth filled him with vigor and offered an indescribable jolt of pleasure, better than any other drug he'd tried.

Some addicts snort meth, while others prefer to either inject it, or smoke the drug in an instrument called a gak pipe. Parnell had his own peculiar method of ingestion: he liked to lay the drug out on toilet paper and gobble down the whole pulpy mess. Within seconds, Parnell would be flying high. His buzz would last for hours, even days, at a time.

On meth, Parnell felt invincible and cocky, like a star athlete about to enter a big game. He could stay awake for days on end without feeling tired. Methamphetamine made life tremendously exciting.

However, what goes up must come down, and coming off a meth high is an unpleasant experience. Most addicts try to avoid it, but eventually sleep overtakes even the most committed meth user. Parnell had his own routine for rest and recuperation. Whenever the drug burned him out to the point where he could barely get out of bed, Parnell would phone in sick to work. He'd sleep for a few days, then begin gulping down meth again.

Parnell could get away with this behavior because he belonged to a union with a generous medical leave policy. He was also an experienced addict. A meth user for years, Parnell knew how to work the system to his advantage.

Parnell first encountered crank at age 21, when he was working construction in Dallas, Texas. Even at this stage, Parnell was something of an old hand when it came to getting high. He'd already sampled marijuana, alcohol, prescription pills, and cocaine, among other intoxicants. A rotten childhood was not the cause; Parnell's upbringing had been relatively normal. He just liked drugs and took lots of them.

In Dallas, Parnell hung around some rather disreputable characters, who were into meth. When he was offered some, Parnell didn't hesitate. His first meth experience was an eye-opener, literally. Nothing he'd taken before prepared him for this drug. It offered a bigger kick than cocaine at a fraction of the price. It was powerful stuff and Parnell loved it.

Following his first taste, Parnell soon acquired a full-blown methamphetamine addiction.

In some ways, his habit actually helped rather than hindered him on the job; jacked up on meth, Parnell could put in 18-hour days at the construction site. When he wasn't working, Parnell got stoned and hung out with fellow dopers and drinkers.

Parnell soon became acquainted with "tweaking"—the result of staying awake for too long while on speed. The combined effects of lack of sleep and the drugs push addicts into a semi-psychotic state, where fantasy and reality blur and hallucinations fill their minds and ears. Tweakers tend to be paranoid and moody. They can go from euphoria to an insane rage in the blink of an eye. Even other addicts are wary of tweakers, who have a tendency towards unprovoked violence. Needless to say, police tend to be wary, too.

Throughout the rest of his 20s and into his early 30s, Parnell continued to work while taking meth. He traveled about the United States, somewhat aimlessly, and in the early 1990s, served some time in an Oklahoma prison for selling marijuana. At some point after that, Parnell moved back to his hometown of Martin, Tennessee. He found a job at a tire factory across the state line and continued to take drugs.

He married a woman named Amy and had several children. At his peak, Parnell was pulling in $35,000 a year from his job. He augmented this income by dealing pot and meth. It was enough to keep his family clothed and fed, while keeping him in drugs. But eventually, Parnell's speed habit caught up with him.

In 2000, at age 33, he tried to commit suicide. It was his first serious attempt. He had been feeling depressed, anxious, and awful. Severe suicidal thoughts kept entering his mind. Tying a rope around his neck and trying to hang himself seemed like a logical thing to do. When his suicide bid failed, Parnell returned to working in the tire plant, raising his kids, and gobbling down ungodly amounts of meth.

As Parnell's meth addiction grew in scope

and intensity, his already fragile mental state started to strain and fray. Staying awake for days on end didn't help. Carrying a rifle around the home, on the other hand, did. Whenever his paranoia overwhelmed him, Parnell would take a few pot shots in his backyard. No one in small-town Tennessee would be alarmed by the sound of occasional rifle-fire.

The neighbors may not have noticed his deteriorating condition, but Parnell's wife, Amy, did. Her husband's addiction had reached a state where he was a danger to himself and the family. In early 2003, Amy said she'd had enough. She wanted to leave him and take the kids. A more sober man might not have been surprised. As it was, Parnell was devastated. With his increasingly tenuous grip on reality slipping away, he grabbed his rifle and told Amy to lie in bed with him. Amy did as he said.

With Amy at his side, Parnell placed the muzzle of his gun under his chin. He pulled the trigger, blowing off most of his facial features.

Splattered with her husband's blood, Amy was in hysterics. Eventually, she managed to call 911. With his ears ringing from the concussive sound of the shot, Parnell realized he was still alive. The meth coursing through his body was so powerful that his self-inflicted wound hadn't knocked him unconscious.

No one—especially Dave Parnell himself—expected him to live. He had eviscerated his nose, lips, and teeth. His face was literally split down the middle. He could still see, hear, and feel pain, however—the sharpest, most intense pain he'd ever experienced in his life. "I thought I was dying," says a surgically reconstructed Parnell today. "I felt my life was slipping out of me ... the pain was so intense it was hard to think of a whole lot of stuff." Parnell lay helpless in his bedroom, waiting to die, as Amy stood by waiting for the ambulance.

Most methamphetamine addicts don't turn rifles on themselves, but it has affected the lives of millions worldwide. According to the United

Nations *World Drug Report 2005,* some 26 million people around the globe tried amphetamines in 2003. Two and a half million of these users lived in Europe, 4.3 million in North and South America, 1.8 million in Africa, and 17.3 million in Asia and Oceania. The most recent National Survey on Drug Use and Health (NSDUH)—a regular barometer of U.S. substance abuse patterns—revealed that 12.3 million Americans have sampled meth at least once in their lives.

These figures pale when compared to the number of people who smoke cigarettes, drink alcohol, or use marijuana. Nonetheless, meth has alarmed health experts, policy-makers, and police. This is because methamphetamine— as Parnell can attest—has the ability to mess users up more quickly than almost any other substance on the planet.

In July 2005, the National Association of Counties (NACo) released a grim report entitled, "The Meth Epidemic in America." The report was based on the results of a survey done for NACo with county law officers across the United States. When asked what illegal drug was causing the most problems in their towns, the vast majority of police officers cited methamphetamine. Meth garnered more votes than heroin, cocaine, and marijuana combined. The NACo report concluded, "Meth is the leading drug-related local law enforcement problem in the country." It's a sentiment shared by the National Conference of State Legislatures. In early 2004, the National Conference issued a briefing paper that labeled meth "the fastest growing drug threat in America."

Certainly David Parnell, lying faceless in his bedroom, would agree. When the police and paramedics showed up in response to Amy's frantic calls, they gave Parnell little chance of surviving. "They wrote me off for dead," he recalls. Parnell was rushed to a hospital where he underwent three days of emergency surgery. When he awoke, everything was different.

"As soon as I came to, all I could think about was how much mercy Jesus had showed me," he says. Parnell had never been particularly spiritual before, but after almost blowing his brains out, he saw the light. This discovery was compounded by a surprise announcement from Amy: his wife was pregnant again, with their seventh child.

Parnell was alive, but he was badly disfigured. Most of his mouth was gone and he couldn't talk. Writing his thoughts down on a notepad, he let Amy know that he wanted to live. He had been given a second chance, and he was determined to stay straight.

It took a bullet to wake him up, but unlike many of his meth-addled peers, Parnell would never take another hit again.

CHAPTER 2

A Manufactured Poison

ethamphetamine is to the drug world what polyester is to fashion. It's a completely synthetic substance conjured up in laboratories. And, according to Doug Pamenter, creator of one of the Internet's most informative anti-meth sites (*www.crystalrecovery.com*), this makes meth all the more dangerous.

"Meth is not like other drugs, that are refinements of naturally occurring chemicals, such

METH'S CHEMISTRY

Methamphetamine is a psychostimulant also known as d-N, alpha-Dimethylbenzeneethanamine.

Methamphetamine Free Base chemical structure
$C_6H_6CH_2CH(NHCH_3)CH_3$

Percent Composition
Carbon 80.48%; Hydrogen 10.13%; Nitrogen 9.39%

Common brand names and trademarks
Desoxyn (Abbot, USA)
Methampex (Lemmon, USA)
Methedrine (Wellcome, UK)
Temmler (Germany)

as cocaine or heroin," says Pamenter, a former addictions counselor on Canada's west coast. "Meth is more of a poison than a drug. It is a poison that gets the user high. In this sense, meth is more like glue or gas."

Most intoxicants, Pamenter points out, come from Mother Nature: alcohol is made from wheat, barley, and hops, while cigarettes are derived from tobacco plants. Marijuana comes from cannabis buds, cocaine comes from coca leaves, and heroin and morphine trace their origin to opium poppies. This doesn't mean other drugs are safe simply because they're organic. But meth's dangers are compounded because the drug is made from already-toxic chemicals such as drain cleaner, battery acid, lye, camping or lantern fuel, and antifreeze. Making meth (a process known as 'cooking'), much less consuming it, is incredibly dangerous.

Methamphetamine also differs from traditional intoxicants in other ways. While marijuana users are sluggish and lethargic, meth makes users extremely aggressive. Meth offers a very long buzz—12 hours or more—compared to crack cocaine's 10-minute high, Unlike heroin, methamphetamine is cheap: a quarter gram goes for about $20 to $60—a bargain, considering you only need a tiny amount to get high. Unlike alcohol and cigarettes, meth doesn't come with warning labels or quality controls on its manufacture.

Meth floods the brain with the neurotransmitter dopamine, an action which "stimulates brain cells, enhancing mood and body movement," according to the National Institute on

Drug Abuse (NIDA). Put more plainly, it gives users increased alertness and energy. Depending on the mode of consumption, meth's effects are felt almost immediately—within a few seconds of smoking meth and about 30 seconds following injection.

Methamphetamine has the curiously dual effect of either scrambling a user's brain and making it impossible to concentrate, or narrowing their focus so much that they repeat the same task over and over. This is called "teching" and it can include everything from obsessive hair brushing to vacuuming the floor for hours on end. Some meth users report "speed bugs"—the sensation that insects are crawling underneath their flesh. People who experience these hallucinatory infestations often pick at their skin until their arms and legs are bloodied and permanently scarred. Other unpleasant physical effects include dilated pupils, blurred vision, muscle tremors, and sweaty, flushed skin. Addicts tend to be paranoid, fidgety, and non-stop babblers.

COMMON SIDE EFFECTS OF METH

Commonly reported physical symptoms were tiredness (89 percent), loss of appetite (85 percent), dehydration (73 percent), and jaw clenching (73 percent). Also reported were headaches, muscle pains, shortness of breath, and tremors. The most frequently reported psychological symptoms were mood swings (80 percent), sleep problems (78 percent), anxiety, difficulty concentrating, depression, and paranoia (each about 70 percent), plus hallucinations, episodes of aggression, and violence.

Source: Dr. Rawson, Dr. Jerome Jaffe, and Dr. Walter Ling referring to symptoms experienced by meth users entering treatment in Australia.

Many addicts suffer from a condition called "meth mouth"—extremely advanced tooth decay. In this state, some users' teeth are rotted right down to their gum line. There are various theories as to why this happens. It's believed smoking meth leaves a film on teeth that increases the pace of rot. In addition, heavy meth users tend to take a laissez-faire attitude toward hygiene and dental care, avoiding baths and toothbrushes for weeks at a time. Users often crave sweets or sugary drinks as well. Finally, methamphetamine dries the mouth out, which further hastens tooth decay. Beyond cavities, meth puts users at risk of stroke, heart failure, and brain impairment. Respiratory problems, irregular heartbeat, and anorexia are other unpleasant effects.

It has yet to be determined if meth's impact on the brain is permanent, or if users can eventually recover full brain function. "Animal research going back more than 20 years shows that high doses of methamphetamine damage neuron cell-endings [in the brain]," states NIDA. "Dopamine- and serotonin-containing neurons do not die after methamphetamine use, but their nerve endings ('terminals') are cut back and regrowth appears to be limited."

Dr. Rawson, who also serves as associate director of the University of California in Los Angeles (UCLA) Integrated Substance Abuse Program, takes a more nuanced view. "For the most part, brain dysfunction caused by meth is reversible but takes six to 12 months," he says. "With some severe long-term injection users, damage may be permanent." Taking methamphetamine often leads to a host of other problems. People on meth often rely on other intoxicants—such as alcohol, sedatives, and opiates—to take the edge off their high. This practice enormously increases the risk of an overdose.

Meth is often the trigger for extremely unsafe behavior, from reckless driving to super-charged sex. While heroin and marijuana put the libido to sleep, methamphetamine can act as a high-potency aphrodisiac. When suitably aroused, meth users tend to have frequent unprotected sex with multiple partners. This aspect of the drug has had particularly serious consequences in gay communities, a subgroup in which methamphetamine use flourishes. A study by the Los Angeles Gay and Lesbian Center looked at the sex and drug habits of nearly 20,000 men. The study found that one-third of all gay men who tested positive for HIV in L.A. in 2004, reported using meth.

Meth users who inject the drug also expose themselves to blood-borne HIV, spread by sharing dirty needles. Many cities have needle exchange programs in which addicts can drop off old syringes an pick up new ones. Needle exchange was originally aimed at heroin users, and the efficacy of such programs on meth addicts hasn't been fully studied.

Likewise, the long-term impact of meth abuse on developing fetuses is unclear. Drug analysts are reluctant to use the label "meth babies" to describe the progeny of female users. In the 1980s, officials were quick to write off the children of crack-addled moms as hopelessly impaired. As it turned out, the impairment of "crack babies" wasn't as bad as originally thought, but the term persists nonetheless. Still, it's safe to say that mixing meth and motherhood is a bad idea. "Pregnancies of methamphetamine-addicted mothers can produce birth defects, low birth weight, attention deficit disorder, and other behavior disorders," reads the National Association of Counties (NACo) "Meth Epidemic in America" report. The ancillary effects of heavy meth use, such as poor eating habits, lack of sleep, stress, and violence—not to mention alcohol and cigarette use—are also bad news for unborn babies.

Of course, no one takes methamphetamine for the negative side effects. Addicts report that the pleasurable aspects of the drug are so overwhelming that decayed teeth, extreme weight loss, and hallucinations about speed bugs seem like petty concerns by comparison. "Meth is better than sex, not because it's like 10 orgasms or anything silly like that, but because it rewards the pleasure centers in your brain more," says Red, a former meth addict, dealer, and cooker from Santa Cruz, California. "Imagine your sex drive multiplied by 10, and call it a meth drive."

But none of this could have been predicted by the scientists who invented it. Meth comes from the amphetamine family tree. First synthesized in Germany in 1887, amphetamine acts like an artificial version of adrenaline—the hormone that kicks in during times of stress—flooding the body with energy. The German scientists who discovered amphetamine had no idea what to do with their new drug. They put it on the shelf and forgot about it. Over the decades, other scientists around the world continued to tinker with amphetamine. The end result was the creation of methamphetamine in a Japanese lab in 1919.

So what is meth? Meth is speed plus; it contains two more hydrogen atoms and one more carbon atom than run-of-the-mill amphetamine. This slight chemical difference makes meth much stronger than its parent drug.

By the late 1920s, scientists determined that amphetamine enlarged nasal and bronchial passages. Delighted to have finally found a use for amphetamine, chemists called the drug a decongestant and packaged it for commercial sale. People could buy speed-based products in pharmacies, without prescriptions. Along the way, a few users noticed that their new decongestant had the curious effect of keeping them awake all night. A growing number of people—including students, truck drivers, farmers, and shift-workers in factories—began taking amphetamine as a pick-me-up to ward off sleep.

Major corporations were soon involved in the speed business: in 1932, the Smith, Kline & French pharmaceutical company began to sell over-the-counter amphetamine inhalers under the brand name Benzedrine. These inhalers were designed to combat stuffy noses. In 1940, Burroughs Wellcome put out a commercial version of methamphetamine, which the company called Methedrine. It was sold as a diet aid and energy-booster.

The military was quick to take note of amphetamine's energizing qualities. Soldiers on both sides of World War II went into battle jacked up on the stuff. According to legend,

Japanese kamikazes (suicidal pilots who deliberately crashed their planes into American ships) and Nazi panzer troops took huge doses of meth to bolster their courage. Hitler himself was rumored to be an amphetamine addict.

After the war ended, amphetamine and methamphetamine continued to be liberally doled out by well-meaning physicians and pharmacists. Doctors sometimes prescribed amphetamine as an anti-depressant or a diet aid. In fact, amphetamine helped Japan back on its feet following the devastation of World War II. Millions of workers took "pep pills" so they could put in the long hours needed for their country to regain its industrial might. Japan prospered, but the price was an epidemic of amphetamine use.

A handful of people began using speed for recreational purposes: in his classic 1950s drug tome, *Junky*, legendary outlaw writer William Burroughs describes mixing "bennies" (Benzedrine) with his coffee. But by the mid-1960s, the negative effects of amphetamine had become widely recognized. People began to realize that the drug was highly addictive. In 1965, the U.S. federal government criminalized most non-medical use and production of amphetamine and methamphetamine.

A black market soon emerged, dominated by outlaw biker gangs. Using a precursor substance named phenyl-2-propanone (P2P), bikers both cooked and sold methamphetamine. They stored the drug in the crankcases of their motorcycles, which is how it acquired the nickname "crank."

The amphetamine family of drugs (a broad category that includes meth), however, had a bad reputation, even in the burgeoning drug culture of the day. Amphetamine and methamphetamine were regarded as dirty substances that fried people's brains and caused violent behavior. Meth's association with bike gangs didn't enhance its image. The slogan "Speed Kills" was coined in response to amphetamine-drugs.

DRUG LAWS

The Controlled Substances Act (CSA), Title II of the Comprehensive Drug Abuse Prevention and Control Act of 1970, is the legal foundation of the U.S. government's fight against the abuse of drugs and other substances. This law regulates the manufacture and distribution of narcotics, stimulants, depressants, hallucinogens, anabolic steroids, and chemicals used in the illicit production of controlled substances.

The CSA places all substances that are regulated under existing federal law into one of five schedules. This placement is based upon each substance's medicinal value, harmfulness, and potential for abuse or addiction. Schedule I is reserved for the most dangerous drugs that have no recognized medical use, while Schedule V is the classification used for the least dangerous drugs. Methamphetamine is a Schedule II drug.

In Canada, the importation, production, distribution, and possession of various drugs and substances are governed by the Controlled Drugs and Substances Act (CDSA). Methamphetamine is classified as a Schedule III drug according to this law. While most provinces have adopted the National Drug Schedule model, Alberta has substantially fewer drugs listed in Schedule III. Quebec currently has no plans to adopt the national model.

People who used amphetamine or methamphetamine were called "speed freaks" and were greatly looked down upon.

In 1970, the U.S. Congress rewrote the nation's laws on "controlled substances" (primarily illicit drugs). Some complicated legislative maneuvering ensued, concerning injectable meth over other forms of speed. The end result was that by the early 1970s, both amphetamine and methamphetamine ended up in "Schedule II" of the federal government's new drug law.

Other prominent drugs in this category included barbiturates and cocaine. Schedule II drugs were deemed to have medical value but also a high risk for abuse. People could still buy both amphetamine and methamphetamine, but they required a broad-minded doctor and a prescription. At present, amphetamine is commercially available under the pharmaceutical name Dexedrine. A version of this drug is used by the U.S. military to keep pilots awake and alert. It's also used to treat attention deficit disorder and narcolepsy. Methamphetamine, meanwhile, is sold in pharmaceutical form as Desoxyn. Made by Ovation Pharmaceuticals of Deerfield, Illinois, Desoxyn is also used for attention deficit disorder and narcolepsy, as well as gross obesity. Many doctors remain wary of prescribing meth, however, because of its terrible reputation.

Like most narcotics legislation, the Drug Abuse Regulation and Control Act did little to regulate or control the flow of illegal drugs. Bikers continued to make and sell meth to truckers, factory workers, and fellow criminals.

Until the late 1980s and early 1990s, methamphetamine remained an obscure pleasure. This might have had something to do with the fact the sellers and users of the drug tended to be working-class white people living in rural areas—a population off the media's radar. During the Reagan and George Bush Sr. eras, the press was far more interested in crack cocaine—a substance largely used and sold by African Americans in inner cities.

Crack received a great deal of coverage because it was addictive, damaging, and easy to report. Crack presented the press with a juicy racial angle that allowed pundits to pontificate and sensationalize. To get a hot story on crack, reporters merely took a trip downtown. Reporting on methamphetamine, on the other hand, meant driving out to

CRACK COCAINE

Crack cocaine is a highly addictive and powerful stimulant, derived from powdered cocaine. It emerged in the mid-1980s. It produces an immediate high and is easy and inexpensive to produce—rendering it readily available and affordable. Crack typically is available as rocks, which are white or off-white, and vary in size and shape. It is nearly always smoked: the term "crack" refers to the crackling sound heard when it is heated. It is a Schedule II drug in the United States and a Schedule I drug in Canada.

rural labs, usually located far from major media centers, and interviewing hillbilly dealers and redneck addicts.

Away from the gaze of the major media, methamphetamine became increasingly popular. This was largely due to several near-simultaneous developments. At some point in the late 1980s, meth cookers discovered that the chemical ephedrine made a much better precursor than phenyl-2-propanone (P2P). Ephedrine was easier to cook with and provided a more potent kick. Then, the Internet arrived. Meth recipes that were once closely guarded became available for anyone to download. Using web-based, ephedrine-laced recipes, amateur cookers began churning out huge amounts of super-strong meth. By the mid-1990s, the once marginal drug had suddenly gone mainstream.

In 1997, 4.5 percent of Americans age 12 and up who responded to the National Household Survey on Drug Abuse (NHSDA) reported lifetime non-medical use of stimulants (a category that includes meth). By 2001, that number had risen to 7.1 percent.

According to a September 2005 bulletin by the Substance Abuse and Mental Health Services Administration (SAMHSA), roughly 12 million Americans age 12 or older have tried meth at least once in their lifetime. Some 1.4 million adults (0.6 percent of the U.S. population) reported past-year meth use in 2004—a rate that has remained stable since 2002. The age of people trying the drug for the first time, meanwhile, has been inching upwards. "The average age at first use among new users was 18.9 years in 2002, 20.4 years in 2003, and 22.1 years in 2004," SAMHSA says.

The sharp increase in meth use since the mid-1990s has been accompanied by an equally abrupt increase in arrests and rehabilitation program admissions. "In 1993, the treatment admission rate for primary amphetamine abuse in the United states was 14 admissions per 100,000 persons aged 12 or older," states Dr. Rawson's study on amphetamine-related disorders. "By 1999, the treatment admission rate for primary amphetamine abuse in the United States as a whole had increased to 32 per 100,000 persons aged 12 or older. Thirteen states had amphetamine admission rates of at least 55 per 100,000 and eight of these had rates of 100 per 100,000 or more."

Treatment rates continue to grow apace in the new millennium; 104,500 meth addicts entered publicly funded drug rehabilitation programs in the United States in 2002, a 119 percent increase from 1995. According to the White House Office of National Drug Control Policy (ONDCP), in 2002, slightly more than half of all users entering methamphetamine treatment in the United States were male. Three-quarters were white. At present, criminal justice referrals account for roughly one-half of all meth-related treatment admissions. The typical criminal justice referral goes like this: a meth user is arrested by police and taken to court. There, they are given a choice—rehab or jail.

The use of speed isn't confined to the United States: the 2004 Canadian Addiction Survey found that 6.4 percent of respondents age 15 or older had used amphetamines at least once. Past-year use was relatively low, however, hovering around one percent. In Europe, estimated past year use of amphetamine among adults was also around one percent.

WORLDWIDE METH ABUSE

The World Health Organization estimates 35 million people worldwide use methamphetamine, making it the #2 illicit drug in the world, second only to cannabis.

Methamphetamine is a major problem in Asia, particularly in Thailand and the Philippines. In the Philippines, meth is known as "shabu." Of 7,720 drug treatment admissions in the Philippines in 2003, nearly 90 percent were for methamphetamine abuse. In some regions of the country, an estimated 5.5 percent of the population regularly uses the drug.

Epidemic during the 1990s, methamphetamine use in Thailand has begun to taper off.

Recent meth use (use within a few months of participating in the research survey) stood at 2.4 percent of the population of Thailand in 2001. A tough law enforcement crack-down saw that figure tumble dramatically to 0.2 percent

METH HOT SPOTS

U.S. states with highest increases in meth-related arrests include: Arizona, Arkansas, California, Florida, Indiana, Louisiana, Minnesota, Nevada, New Mexico, Ohio, Oklahoma, Oregon, South Carolina, Tennessee, Utah, Washington, and Wyoming.

in 2003. However, this figure may have more to do with fear of reporting meth use than an actual reduction in users. "Methamphetamine remained the number one drug for which Thais received treatment in 2003, followed by heroin, cannabis, and opium," notes a 2005 report by the United Nations Office on Drugs for East Asia and the Pacific.

Meth is what sociologists call "criminogenic." Put more plainly, people under its influence often commit violent crimes, such as assault, rape, and murder. Alcohol and cocaine are also criminogenic, as anyone who has experienced a barroom brawl or nightclub melee can attest. Marijuana and heroin are not; people high on these drugs are usually too docile to pick fights. Heroin users may turn to robbery to support their habit, but they're usually in withdrawal when they do so. Likewise, cigarette smokers are generally only ornery when denied a nicotine fix.

The police officers that responded to the National Association of Counties (NACo) survey were certainly aware of meth's crime-causing properties. Of the officers in the NACo study, 70 percent said robberies or burglaries had increased in their jurisdictions due to methamphetamine use. As well, 62 percent blamed meth for an increase in domestic violence, while 53 percent said the same for simple assault.

CHAPTER 3

Cooking and Cleaning

Methamphetamine's sudden explosion in use was matched by major changes in the marketing of the drug. During the 1990s, the outlaw biker gangs that had previously controlled meth distribution were muscled aside by what the ONDCP refers to as "Mexico-based trafficking groups."

"Mexico-based trafficking groups [currently] dominate the market for many reasons, including their ability to obtain large quantities of the chemicals needed to produce the drug, their access to established smuggling and distribution networks, and their control over 'super labs' (laboratories capable of producing in excess of 10 pounds [4.5 kg] of methamphetamine in one 24-hour production cycle)," says the ONDCP.

While the Mexican mob might control the wholesale end of the market, meth's availability is largely predicated on small-time 'cookers' and dealers. "Unlike most drugs that are imported from other countries, methamphetamine can be made by just about anyone in home 'labs,'" states Dr. Rawson in an unpublished paper written with Rachel Gonzales.

Red agrees: "Making meth requires the equivalent of a high school chemistry education, or another cook to teach you." Born in 1984 in Pittsburgh, but raised in Santa Cruz, Red spent a few short years in the methamphetamine trade, working primarily as an independent operator. "I went years without a job or a real home," he recalls. "I lived in people's houses [in exchange] for dope. I made money for gas and food and everything else I had by selling dope." He claims to have figured out how to make meth on his own, with the help of a buddy who was happy to experiment with various recipes. Red also picked up some pointers from "a free online refresher course" on basic organic chemistry.

For those who failed high school chemistry, recipe books such as *Secrets of Methamphetamine Manufacture,* come in handy. The 213-page paperback is written by one "Uncle Fester"—the nom de plume of a middle-aged chemist named Steve Preisler. His tome is available for $34.95 through such alternative booksellers as Loompanics Unlimited. But *Secrets* is also listed on mainstream Internet book-buying web sites.

"For nearly 20 years now, I have been training champions, the champions of the field of clandestine chemistry. This book is their training ground," writes Fester/Preisler in *Secrets' www.amazon.com* listing. "I cover virtually every possible method of making that 'food of the God's' [*sic*]—meth—along with how to make it from commonplace materials."

A California news service investigation conducted in 2000 revealed that Preisler lives in Green Bay, Wisconsin, has degrees from Milwaukee's Marquette University, and is employed as an electroplating chemist. He has two children, thinks the "War on Drugs" is a travesty, and says governments have no right to ban chemicals based on their perceived danger to the public. Fester/Preisler's libertarian stance is reflected in his choice of book topics. In addition to *Secrets*, his repertoire includes titles such as *Home Workshop Explosives, Practical LSD Manufacture,* and *Bloody Brazilian Knife Fighting Techniques.* Fester/Preisler takes a rather casual stance towards the radical nature of his books. "When not working the dayjob [*sic*] or raising my kids, I research the problems confronting clandestine chemists and train for running marathons," he writes.

Most of the dozen or so critics who have written reviews of *Secrets* for *www.amazon.com* seem dazzled: "This book is an excellent resource for people who are either eager to start making meth, or just want to know how it's made without any intention of making it," writes an anonymous critic. "Uncle Fester is a pioneer and a brilliant writer who keeps the readers' interest from page to page." A less impressed reviewer named Scott, from Phoenix, Arizona, complains "the book lacked proper illustrations." And yet another online critic suggests that Fester hand out Uzi sub-machine guns along with copies of his tome, considering the harm his work might cause.

People who would rather get their recipes for free can turn to the Internet, which is packed with meth-making information. Like recipes for moonshine circulated during Prohibition, the veracity of these online recipes is questionable. In fact, one recipe tracked down by this writer contains the following disclaimer: "Success rate is extremely low and process is very dangerous." Underneath this helpful warning is a detailed explanation of how to synthesize ephedrine from Sudafed, followed by meth cooking instructions. Still, it's clear that enough Internet recipes work to keep cookers in business.

Cookers also benefit from the fact that the actual science behind making meth is relatively straightforward. With the exception of one extra oxygen atom, ephedrine, a precursor substance of illicit meth, is chemically similar to methamphetamine. To make meth, cookers have to get rid of this oxygen atom (or "reduce it" in chemistry lingo). Doing so involves bathing ephedrine with red phosphorus, hydriodic acid, and other chemicals.

Ephedrine used to be legal and easy to obtain, but in the late 1980s, U.S. Congress passed legislation that greatly restricted its use. Unfazed, cookers simply turned to pseudoephedrine, a substance found in common cold medications, such as Sudafed. Enormous amounts of sinus medications are needed to glean enough pseudoephedrine to make meth. Red phosphorus comes from the striker pads of common household matches. Other ingredients required for the manufacture of meth are iodine, ether, anhydrous ammonia, acetone, and lye. Necessary lab equipment includes measuring cups, lab grade glass flasks and beakers, pH sticks, Pyrex trays, eyedroppers, and glass stir rods.

Many of the chemicals used to make meth are both highly toxic and very dangerous, especially when mixed together. Lab explosions, clouds of poison, and eyeball-melting infernos are some of the vocational hazards associated with making meth. The web site *www.crystal-recovery.com* contains a large selection of color photographs of cookers whose recipes backfired. Some of these unlucky souls are charred beyond human recognition, while others boast huge acid burns and scorch marks on their flesh.

A cover story in *Newsweek* ("America's Most Dangerous Drug," August 8, 2005) also highlights the dangers of making meth. A sidebar in the article details a pair of youthful meth users who survived horrendous lab mishaps. Their melted flesh makes them look like victims of a napalm attack. Less subtle, but potentially just as damaging to cookers, is the long-term effect of breathing in toxic vapors all day.

The dangers of making meth didn't stop Red in his pursuit of profits and adventure. Unlike many cookers, he was at least cognizant of the perils of his chosen trade. "I never worked in a [place] that had a gas stove, a water heater or anything else with a pilot light," he says. Working in such an environment was to invite an explosion.

People who grow marijuana face a number of restrictions on acquiring the necessary equipment. Police have been known to raid garden supply stores or outlets selling grow lights, if they are suspected of being involved in the drug trade. Red, on the hand, never experienced any problems buying supplies and equipment for his meth lab operations. "Everything could be purchased from a Safeway [supermarket] and a hardware store ... except iodine, which you buy at a farm supply store," he says.

Starting a meth lab doesn't involve a massive financial investment either; according to Red, a beginner cook can purchase sufficient equipment and supplies for under $200, "if they know what they're doing." According to the Drug Enforcement Administration (DEA), a pound (0.5 kg) of finished meth powder can sell for between $1,600 and $45,000 on the street while an ounce (28 g) goes for $270 to $5,000. A pound (0.5 kg) of "ice" (crystal methamphetamine) sells for $6,000 to $70,000, while an ounce (28 g) sells for between $500 and $3,100. Prices are generally lower in California than in the states along the eastern seaboard.

Red typically cooked meth in residences belonging to his drug buddies. "I would approach customers of mine who I came to trust, who had stable housing," he says. "If they agreed, I set up my gear in their house and cooked there. I never let people come over while I worked." Red could get away with such arrangements because the equipment and supplies needed to manufacture meth are relatively portable. Unlike marijuana grow operations or coca and opium farms, meth labs don't take up a lot of space. This rule doesn't apply to "super-labs," which do require a large surface area.

While Red set up shop in customers' residences, other cooks prefer to use cheap motel rooms, preferably located in the middle of nowhere. Warehouses and barns are also popular spots—anywhere that's far from prying eyes.

Once rare, illicit meth labs are now commonplace. "Between 1992 and 2004, the number of clandestine lab-related cleanups [in the United States] increased from 394 to nearly 17,000," Joseph Rannazzisi, deputy chief, office of Enforcement Operations for the DEA, testified

HOW TO TELL IF THERE'S A METH LAB IN YOUR NEIGHBORHOOD

- Strong solvent chemical odor (cat urine, alcohol, ether)
- Blacked out windows
- Large number of gas cans
- Excessive traffic coming and going at odd hours, particularly at night
- Unusually large amounts of trash, possibly containing odd items such as antifreeze bottles, cold decongestant packages, drain cleaner, etc.
- Laboratory equipment such as glass tubes, beakers, Bunsen burners, funnels, chemical glassware, plastic tubing, pressurized tanks, and cylinders
- Large quantities of glassware, such as mason jars
- Heavily guarded premises
- Coffee filters with red stains or soaked in alcohol and ether
- Excessive amounts of hot plates, pressure cookers, or electric skillets
- Large number of empty blister packaging used for over-the-counter medication
- Plastic bottles with the bottoms cut out
- Chemical cans or drums in the yard, with blacked out labels
- Iodine or chemical-stained bathroom and kitchen fixtures
- Explosions

Source: www.crystalrecovery.com

before Congress in November 2004.

America's meth-lab epicenter is not New York City or Los Angeles, but rather the heartland state of Missouri. Between 2002 and 2004, law officers raided an estimated 8,000 meth labs, equipment caches, and toxic dumps in Harry S. Truman's home state.

Meth labs do terrible things to homes, neighborhoods, and the environment. "For every pound of methamphetamine produced, about six pounds of toxic waste is left behind," reads the meth briefing paper published by the National Conference of State Legislatures.

This toxic goo—like the chemicals used to cook meth—is highly dangerous. "Many of the contaminants present during meth's cooking process can be harmful if someone is exposed to them," reads a paper posted at *www.kci.org*. "These contaminants can cause health problems, including respiratory problems, skin and eye irritation, headaches, nausea and dizziness."

Wise cookers take precautions against such

contaminants; Red, for example, recommends using a respirator with a filter, otherwise "you get dizzy and confused when there's too many fumes." Most police officers, however, don't usually carry respirators with them when on patrol, which makes lab-busting a risky proposition. "Acute (short-term) exposures to high concentrations of some of these chemicals, such as those law enforcement officers face when they first enter a lab, can cause severe health problems, including lung damage and burns to different parts of the body," reads *www.kci.org.*

Formerly the Koch Crime Institute of Kansas, and now a self-proclaimed, "anti-meth site," *www.kci.org* offers a detailed analysis of the steps needed to clean a meth lab. Before anything else, the site has to be aired out, preferably for a few days. Exhaust fans can help in this regard. Once the location has been thoroughly aired, lab equipment and material must be carefully removed. This is typically done by either police officers or trained experts wearing

Tyvek protective suits, respirators, thick-soled boots, and industrial-strength rubber gloves.

"Absorbent materials, such as carpeting, drapes, clothing, etc. can accumulate vapors that are dispersed through the air during the cooking process," reads *www.kci.org*. "They also may collect dust and powder from the chemicals involved in the manufacturing process. It is recommended that these materials be disposed of, especially if an odor or discoloration is present." Surface areas, including walls, ceilings, and counters have to be thoroughly cleaned, a process that can entail tearing out floorboards and drywall. It's recommended that cleaners check a site's drains; cookers often dump unneeded chemicals down sinks and toilets. When this occurs, the result is a clogged up septic system that continues to give off dangerous fumes.

Once all of the equipment has been removed, surface areas cleaned, and plumbing examined, *www.kci.org* recommends repainting, "especially in areas where contamination

METH IN CANADA

Canada's western provinces, particularly Alberta and British Columbia, are worst hit by the country's growing meth problem. The number of clandestine methamphetamine laboratories seized across Canada rose from 4 in 1998 to 37 in 2003. In 2004, the Royal Canadian Mounted Police reported 30 busts in the province of BC alone.

In 2003, new legislation was introduced in Canada aimed at stemming the flow of Canadian chemical shipments to meth labs in the United States.

Source: CBC's The Fifth Estate

was found or suspected. If there is any remaining contamination that cleaning did not remove, painting the surface puts a barrier between the contamination and anyone who may come in contact with those surfaces."

Lab equipment and toxic fumes sometimes aren't the only things left behind in a meth lab. "According to the El Paso Intelligence Center (EPIC), over 3,000 children were present during the seizure of clandestine laboratories nationwide in 2003," Rannazzisi said during his Congressional testimony.

A grim bulletin issued January 2005 by the Minnesota Department of Human Services offers child protection workers instruction on how to deal with children found in such places. "If the child had minimum exposure to the contaminants, wrap him/her in a sheet and remove his/her shoes before transporting the child to the foster home," reads the bulletin. "If the lab site was inside the child's home, the child may carry a larger amount of contaminants on their clothing and body, so a number of steps should be taken. Law enforcement may have set up a decontamination tent where contaminated clothing can be removed and a portable shower is available."

With or without the presence of children, cleaning up meth sites costs a lot of money. "After law enforcement officials seize a lab, the average cost of cleanup is about $5,000, but it can climb to as much as $150,000 for large-scale labs," states the National Conference of State Legislatures paper.

Who picks up the tab is a major sore point. Technically, the property owner is responsible for any mess incurred on his or her real estate.

However, if the property owner pleads ignorance or poverty, the issue of culpability might have to be resolved in the courts. Meanwhile, the seized meth lab sits dormant but emitting dangerous fumes. In the end, local counties often have to shoulder the immediate costs of cleanup. Counties also have to pay for police officers to guard lab sites until cleaners can arrive. In a locale with lots of meth labs and a tiny police force, this can be an expensive proposition.

Local law authorities are angry at the federal government's apathy towards meth. Until recently, government agencies focused most of their drug-fighting energy on other drugs, particularly marijuana. In November 2002, for example, "drug czar" John Walters, who heads the ONDCP, fired off a letter to U.S. prosecutors. It states, "Nationwide, no drug matches the threat posed by marijuana."

County police beg to differ; of the police officers who responded to the NACo survey,

58 percent said that methamphetamine was the largest drug problem in their jurisdiction. "Meth was followed by cocaine (19%), marijuana (17%) and heroin (3%) as the number one drug problem," the report reads. Local police know that while not without its negative effects, cannabis is hardly in the same league as meth. Cannabis makes people sleepy, lazy, and hazy—minor threats compared with the violent rush triggered by methamphetamine. These points seem lost on federal agencies.

"On the national level, the federal government still considers marijuana as the number one drug problem in America, but county law enforcement officials have a different perspective on this ranking," says the NACo study. At a July 2005 press conference in Washington, D.C., to herald the release of the survey, NACo executive director Larry Naake echoed this sentiment: "We'd like to call on the administration to put the same kind of emphasis on meth abuse as they have on marijuana."

Cannabis is the most widely used illicit drug, which is one reason why Washington is fixated on it. In fact, marijuana has been the linchpin in the federal government's War on Drugs for decades. Drug warriors bent on fighting marijuana find it difficult to suddenly change enemies in the midst of battle. Thanks to NACo and other organizations, however, government officials have finally clued in to the menace posed by meth. "I think we would all agree that methamphetamine is the most destructive, dangerous, terrible drug that's come along in a long time," stated Scott Burns, White House Deputy Director for State and Local Affairs, ONDCP, in July 2005.

That same month, in a speech to district attorneys, U.S. Attorney General Alberto Gonzales upped the ante even more. "In terms of damage to children and to our society, meth is now the most dangerous drug in America," said Gonzales. These remarks signaled a turning point in the war on meth. The White House has finally removed its blinders and acknowledged that methamphetamine is drug problem number one in the United States. Whether the government has anything useful to contribute to the battle against meth, remains unclear.

CHAPTER 4

The Faces of Meth

inding religion was a life-changing experience for David Parnell. His newfound spirituality didn't do anything to speed up the physical healing process, however. After shooting off half his face while in a state of meth-induced paramoia, Parnell's recovery was a result of time, patience, and a lot of plastic surgery. During his recovery in the hospital, Parnell communicated by writing notes on a pad. In this manner, Parnell told his wife, Amy, that he had a new ambition: once he was healed enough to speak, he wanted to "go around and tell the truth about drugs."

After a month in the hospital, Parnell was deemed sufficiently healed to be discharged. He went home and spent another month in bed, trying to regain his strength. Parnell needed it; he was determined to kick methamphetamine once and for all. Parnell wasn't taking the drug any more, but hadn't completely beaten his addiction either. After a few weeks in bed, Parnell entered an outpatient drug treatment program at a local hospital. He felt cravings, but didn't give in to them. Mostly, he just felt tired. He could sleep 12 hours and still be exhausted.

Over the next two years, he endured extensive plastic surgery. Parnell estimated he had at least 18 major operations, and may need more. His mouth and nose were completely rebuilt. "I've got 30 plates that hold my face together," he says. "When they worked on my nose, they built it from my forehead." Workplace insurance covered a large portion of his medical bills, but Parnell says he still owes "thousands."

Parnell says his grandfather was a preacher, but he never felt particularly religious until his failed suicide attempt. During his recovery, Parnell began going to church. He was eventually baptized in the Baptist faith and contemplated what to do with his life now that it was on the right track.

* * *

Rashelle Chaplin didn't shoot herself in the face, but she was reduced to living in her car, thanks to meth. Now a well-known presence in the online recovery community, 34-year-old Chaplin was born in Akron, Ohio. Like Parnell—and the vast majority of meth users—she's white.

Chaplin reports a normal childhood; her parents were "loving, caring people who went out of their way" to provide affection and a supportive home environment. Nicotine and alcohol are the first drugs she has any memory of. Her mother and father smoked cigarettes and occasionally "had a few cocktails" to wind down at the end of the day. Neither of her parents were problem drinkers, she says.

Chaplin was introduced to illegal drugs as a young teen. She began smoking marijuana, then quickly moved on to other intoxicants. In 1993, when she was 22 years old and working in a bar, Chaplin used methamphetamine for the first time. She describes the experience as "euphoric and enlightening. [You] go-go-go and obsess over details."

"I had great concentration, felt great about myself and didn't want to sleep. I didn't, for three days," she continues. At first, her meth use was strictly confined to leisure time, taking the drug made weekends more exciting. Soon, though, she was taking meth during the week as well. Eventually, Chaplin was using meth all the time, and going on sleepless drug "runs" for days on end. Fifteen days in a row was the longest she ever stayed awake. Chaplin managed to stay employed, but turned most of her paycheck over to drug dealers, spending $250 to $500 per week on meth.

"During the last few months of my overpowering addiction, I had lost about seven [clothing] sizes within one to two months," she writes on her web site *www.methmadness.com.* "I was barely sleeping or eating and working 13 hour shifts at work."

"By the winter of 1997/98, I was literally dying inside," she reports. "My husband was an abuser of meth too, and I was the victim of spousal abuse, physically and mentally … "

She was also a physical wreck. "By the time I had gone the duration of my abuse, I had translucent skin, bloody scabs and pick marks all over my body," states Chaplin. "My kidneys were failing, I had brittle hair and nails, paranoia, hallucinations … weak muscles and a very low immune system."

On July 1, 1998, she decided to quit. This decision involved leaving her place of work, her friends, and her husband. Chaplin ended up living in a Chevy Cavalier, with almost no money to her name. She didn't book herself into a rehabilitation program, taking the far riskier choice of kicking meth all by herself. Chaplin rode out her withdrawal symptoms on the seat of a car, while contemplating life as a street person and an addict.

* * *

Jennifer Romano of Mabank, Texas, got involved with methamphetamine in spite of having a family member with major substance abuse issues. "I remember thinking in high school I would never do drugs, because they are bad for you and will hurt you," she writes in an Internet confession at *www.crystalrecovery.com*. "I remember what other members of my family went through and are still going through with my Uncle Eddy, and his drug addictions. He would steal anything from anyone to get money for drugs ... He stole painkillers from his own mother (my grandmother) before she passed away. She had MS [multiple sclerosis] and he stole her morphine."

In the late 1990s, Romano began smoking marijuana and cigarettes, and drinking alcohol. By 1998, she was dating a man she identifies as "Jr." She lived with her new boyfriend at his mother's place and dabbled in cocaine and speed. At first, Romano and her partner were content to snort meth. Then, they experimented with smoking the drug off aluminum foil or in a glass pipe. Finally, Romano graduated to injecting the drug. This produced particularly euphoric results.

"I remember it like it was yesterday. Oh, the rush of it! The way it made me feel ... anyone who has shot meth or coke knows what I am talking about. The feeling you get ... it warms your body from head to toe ... the taste in the back of your mouth," writes Romano.

In February 1999, Romano and Jr. got their own place. Within weeks, they had their first run-in with police. The trouble began after they evicted a roommate for not paying any bills. The evicted woman called police and said that her former housemates were expecting a huge shipment of speed that evening. The police searched Romano and Jr.'s house, but didn't find any speed. (There was no shipment.) However, police did find some drug paraphernalia and prescription diet pills. Pondimum, the main substance in the diet pills, had been taken off the market and was illegal to possess. "The pills got mixed up in my stuff when we moved out of my parents' house," writes Romano. "Since the pills were in my house, I got charged with possession of a controlled substance. We lost our place to live and moved in with [Jr.'s] mother."

On her 19th birthday—April 16, 1999—Jennifer discovered that she was pregnant.

That September, a heavily pregnant Romano, was put on probation for the Pondimum pills police found in their raid. Romano gave birth to a girl in December of that year, and a few months alter the small family moved into another place of their own. She swore she wouldn't do hard drugs again, but even a new baby and a brush with the law couldn't stop her addiction.

Romano and Jr. hooked up with a meth cooker. "We took him everywhere he needed to go and in return we got free dope," Romano writes. "What a great deal we had going on, or at least, that is what we thought!" Romano and Jr. married in March of 2000. Their thoughtful cooker presented the happy couple with "two eight balls of speed" as a wedding gift. Shortly thereafter, Romano and Jr. were evicted for spending their rent money on dope. Homeless, they moved in with Romano's parents.

That June, Romano was pregnant again. She briefly stopped using meth. Three months later, her husband went to jail for six months.

While he was in jail, Romano began injecting meth on a steady basis. "The night I went into labor, I had shot some speed. [My baby] was born six weeks early, on December 12, 2000. I had meth in my system of course, but when they did the drug test on the baby and her placenta, they found no traces of any drugs. What a miracle!" she writes.

Miracles aside, life for the rapidly expanding family would get worse before it got better. Romano spent time in prison. She attempted suicide, taking enough sleeping pills to kill several grown men. Child Protective Services took her two daughters into custody. After almost two years of ruining her life with methamphetamine, she'd had enough. It was time to separate herself from the meth lifestyle. "I left my husband on 15th of September [2002] ... two days before his birthday," she writes. After her split with Jr., Romano managed to stay clean for awhile, but then relapsed in July of 2003 and again in August 2004. Her latest "clean date" is November 2004.

"I have chosen this drug over everyone—myself, my children, my parents, my lovers and my close friends, all of whom I have hurt in one way or another because of meth," she writes.

"Meth will make your life a living hell ... I have done the "picking" and left sores all over my body. I have had suicidal thoughts on more than one occasion. I thought people were out to get me. I never thought I would do this drug again. I guess the saying 'once an addict, always an addict' is true," she adds.

Romano, however, remains determined to beat the odds. She belongs to Alcoholics Anonymous and Narcotics Anonymous and dreams of one day being completely clean. She takes a philosophical attitude to her drug habit. "I did not destroy my life in one day, a month or even a year. So it is going to take time to put it back together," she writes.

* * *

David M. has gone considerably further in his recovery. He's managed to stay off meth for several years and has embraced his new sober life.

"I was born in Compton, California, in 1952. Compton is a suburb of Los Angeles and located inside the L.A. County line," says David. "My parents were both first-generation Americans of Mexican ancestry ... At the age of three, the family moved from Compton to another suburb of Los Angeles called La Puente."

"Even though we were of Mexican ancestry ... we always lived in all-white neighborhoods. We did not speak Spanish at home and mom did not cook Mexican food," he adds.

Family life, recalls David, "was very crazy. Lots of physical and emotional abuse ... I was a kid who never had friends. They were discouraged by my parents."

David first tried drugs at age 16, shortly after his family moved into the vast suburbs of Orange County. "I was in high school, and determined to have a different life," he recalls. "I started giving a brother and sister who lived in my neighborhood rides to and from school. One day on the way home, they invited me to their house I thought, 'Cool, finally friends'. We got in and they rolled a joint and offered me some."

"I knew in that moment that if I said 'no', I would lose my first new friends," continues David. "So, I was off and running. I actually learned how to smoke cigarettes as a way to practice pot smoking." David was soon sampling other drugs, including LSD and mescaline. Then at age 17, he told his parents he was gay and moved out of the family house to learn hairdressing. It was a vocation he excelled at; by the 1980s, David says he was making a "high five figure" salary cutting hair. By this point, he had largely stopped using drugs, besides "an occasional joint before a movie." He didn't care for alcohol, so it wasn't a big part of his adult life either.

David did enjoy sex and partying, however. He began to explore gay telephone chat lines. He used these phone lines to meet people and arrange sexual rendezvous. In 1994, one of his new contacts invited him to a party in Irwindale, an L.A. suburb. At the party, David was offered some crystal methamphetamine—a more potent variety of the drug. "To be perfectly honest, I had no idea what crystal was," he admits. "I figured it was something like cocaine, which I never liked. Anyway, I left that house after about 20 hours, and that was it. I was hooked. Within three months, I was shooting up."

"I think the longest I went with no sleep was about 11 days. I would use [meth] until I would just pass out for a day or two. Then I would open my eyes and start all over again. I never tried to quit. The first time I stuck a needle in my arm, I knew that was how I was going to die, and that was okay with me," he says.

At his worst, David was shooting up two or three times every day. "I managed to keep my job with all my erratic behavior and scary looks because my boss and my clients thought I was dying of AIDS," he says.

David became HIV positive for real in 1999, as a result of his hard drug use. Whether he contacted the disease from a dirty needle or an infected sex partner, he won't say. It was most likely the latter, as David claims to have been obsessively hygienic when it came to injecting drugs. "This might sound incredible to you, but I was meticulous with my needles and never shared them," he says. "I think you may have found that among intravenous drug users, the ritual is an important part of using. My ritual was to load my syringe with bleach and push it out, doing this twice, then rinsing thoroughly with hot water."

Being fussy about his needles didn't make his personal life any less messy, however. "At my lowest point, I was evicted from an apartment that I had lived in for 14 years," David recalls. "My old and non drug-using friends got together with my sister and talked about my drug problem. Not knowing what to do, they called the police, who had me 51/50'd." California police

code 51/50 allows law enforcement to hospi-
talize a mentally ill person who is a danger to
themselves or the community.

"I was put in a psych ward at County USC
hospital," David continues. "I was in a psych
lock down for two weeks. Within 48 hours of my
release, I had a needle in my arm again." David's
relapse lasted eight months. It ended, only when
a fellow drug user whom he'd had "an on-again,
off-again relationship" with for years, suddenly
decided to go clean.

"When my partner announces that we
have a drug problem and need to quit, I see my
chance to solidify our relationship," David recalls. "I know he can't get sober on his own and
he'll need me to get and stay sober ... [so], I find
a Crystal Meth Anonymous meeting and off we
go. That was Monday night, March 11th, 1999,
and the last time I ever used crystal."

"Was [quitting] easy? I don't think so. Was it
do-able? Absolutely!" David continues. "I never
did rehab or anything else to get sober. For me,

it was meetings, fellowship, and working the steps. In the first six months of recovery, I had quadruple bypass surgery, lost my job, and had my car repossessed."

He stayed clean, however, and made a full recovery. He got a new job that pays considerably less than his previous gig as a salon superstar.

"I make about a fifth of what I used to as a hairdresser. I have a bus pass instead of a new car every three years. I live in a small, single apartment instead of a 1,500-square-foot apartment, and have to think twice about how I spend my money," he reports. "Am I happy? You bet. I have my life back, my old, pre-crystal meth friends back and a wealth of new friends who brought me back from the dead."

* * *

Red, a former meth cooker and user, isn't quite as thrilled to be walking the straight and narrow. Sobriety seems gray and lifeless after the

Technicolor splendor of methamphetamine.

Red first sampled cigarettes, alcohol, and marijuana at age 16. At 17, he was living on his own in a rented Santa Cruz room, having graduated from high school early. Red decided to try a stronger kick. "I thought the idea of 'speed' was cool. I wanted to see what it felt like not to feel sleepy for days on end," he recalls.

Unlike most people interviewed for this book, Red wasn't dazzled by his first encounter with methamphetamine. In fact, he calls the experience "disappointing." "I had never done hard drugs before and expected something more dramatic," Red explains. "I ended up going to sleep about four hours after I first used it—though it was hard. I woke up still high and decided then that I loved it."

After that, he started taking the drug regularly. The longest he stayed awake was five days. Not a terribly long period of time, he concedes, even if he was permanently wired.

"I lived high for months and months on end,

to the point that when I'd get locked up and be forced sober, it felt so strange," he recalls. "I remember telling people it was like a whole different high, being sober, because high was how I was normally."

If being permanently stoned was a thrill, so was cooking meth and leading the drug dealer lifestyle. He describes this period as the "most adventurous time" in his life. "I felt like I had a thousand friends and my life was a constant party, even if they weren't my friends. They just loved the dope and the party was just a bunch of desperate people fulfilling their craving for methamphetamine," says Red. "I remember I never paid for anything when I was dealing. People gave me anything I needed in exchange for dope."

On top of party favors and instant friends, Red also enjoyed the business side of dealing. "I had price wars with people; I took over people's customer bases," he says. "I crave the politics of it—who's your friend; who is loyal enough to spy for you on your competition; who will fight for you if it comes down to it; who is dangerous ... how low do you have to drop your prices if you want to put a rival out of business."

The economics of dealing was nothing, however, compared to the thrill of danger that came with the job. "I remember that I was having trouble holding my control in a trailer park from a rival group," he says. "I ended up showing up there and demanding money I was owed in no uncertain terms from the guy that ran most of the park's business. He got all pissed off because he thought it was disrespectful the way I called him a liar in front of a house full of his people. Some people in San Jose were called who tried to start a fight with my partner and I, as we were on our way to pick up a lot of dope."

"The whole thing culminated in a long, high-speed chase all over town, and their car being smashed up with a baseball bat," he concludes.

Red went clean after being arrested in January 2005, on what he calls "utterly fabricated charges" following what he insists was an illegal search. Now, he's out of the methamphetamine business. Red is currently living in Santa Cruz and "working legally, for the first time in years ... I work as a plumber's assistant. I mostly dig ditches," he says.

It's a boring life, made worse by comparison with his previous employment. "I find myself now feeling like a stimulation junkie. It is hard for me to live this normal life," Red states. "I find myself wanting the drama of [life as a dealer] ... I want to be back where I'm like a celebrity. I want to be running around in the middle of the night dodging the cops. I want to be in charge of a group again, complete with enemies, allies, contacts, and favors owed."

"I think it's like soldiers getting back from war," he says. "After what they've been through, it's hard to feel like all this everyday stuff matters ..."

* * *

Katie Murphy had a considerably less enjoyable time during her brief fling with methamphetamine. Born in Weymouth, Massachusetts in 1981, but raised in suburban Boston, Murphy comes from a large and unhealthy family of seven brothers and three sisters. "I lived my entire childhood on welfare, having to take care of my mother's children while dealing with physical, mental, sexual and emotional abuse from her, her [boyfriend] and my maternal grandmother," she recalls.

She recalls drinking alcohol and smoking marijuana at age 16, but didn't encounter meth until a boyfriend introduced it to her. "My boyfriend had asked [permission] for his good friend to stay with us," says Murphy. "[He said] it was a 'life or death' situation. After she arrived, I learned she had been a heroin addict for two years and was doing meth at our house to ease withdrawal from heroin. She offered [some for me to] smoke ... I didn't really know what it was, but figured, 'why not?'"

Her first experience with methamphet-amine was a positive one: "I was surprised it did keep me up and going like it did. I was happy, having fun, did not feel tired. Had no hangover or withdrawal. It was great."

Murphy says it only took her a couple of days to become addicted. As a steady user, she recalls staying awake for a week at a time. Negative side effects were not long in coming. Soon, Murphy was hallucinating from lack of sleep and the impact of meth on her brain. These hallucinations were both visual and auditory; she recalls hearing imaginary voices talking about her, and seeing imaginary people darting around her house—"complete schizophrenic reactions," she says.

Murphy also felt physically weak and experienced the sensation that her body was rotting. On top of meth, Murphy also dabbled in heroin "and any other drug I could get my hands on." Finally, in the spring of 2005, she flew to Boston, where her brother lived, to kick her addiction.

Like Rashelle Chaplin, she was determined to withdraw from meth on her own. She won her fight with addiction, though, at a high personal cost. "It is extremely difficult to quit meth," she states. "Everything makes you think about it."

Now living in Tucson, Arizona, Murphy is still considering going to a rehabilitation program, if only to strengthen her resolve never to use meth again.

* * *

Prison was the impetus for Abby B. to go clean.

She was born in St. Paul, Minnesota in 1982, and describes her family as "very loving and kind." "My mom and dad are divorced, but they got along," she recalls. "We never saw them argue or have anything bad to say about the other person."

A stepsister introduced Abby B. to cigarettes. "It was 'cool' and 'bad' and something to do," she says. Soon, she graduated to drinking alcohol and smoking marijuana. "I thought that pot and alcohol would make things more fun," she says.

Eventually, Abby sought out new pleasures. "I had a good friend that used meth ... I told him I wanted to try meth," she recalls.

"I don't think there are words in English that can really describe it," Abby says of her first experience with speed in 2001. "I didn't know what to feel, so I didn't know if I was high, but I felt different than I normally do. I was surprised when I realized it was 12 hours later, and I wasn't tired or hungry. It was fun, so I did it again. And again, and again."

Addiction came fast: "I remember deciding to get meth the first two times I used. After that, I didn't decide anything. I had to get meth. That was my option, get meth," says Abby.

She thinks her longest run lasted two weeks, although she isn't entirely clear. Like many methamphetamine users, she says it was difficult to keep track of time when she was high.

At her lowest point, Abby abandoned her job, house, and family and moved to Arizona with some fellow meth addicts. Soon after arriving in the state, she was arrested and went to jail. Forced sobriety was the spur she needed to quit for good.

"I stayed clean while I was in jail and became a member of a 12-step fellowship when I got out," she says. Now living in Minnesota, Abby remains in a 12-step program. She won't say what the program is, other than it is not Crystal Meth Anonymous—the main group of its kind for former meth users.

* * *

Unlike most of the people interviewed for this book, whose addiction led to unemployment, SF Jaye is a prime example of the "functional user"—one who keeps a largely even keel, even while stoned. A denizen of San Francisco (hence the nickname), SF Jaye has posted a tale of his struggle on a personal web site at *http://sfjaye.freewebspace.com/index.html.*

"I graduated from high school in 1962, then served four years in the U.S. Air Force, with numerous awards and an honorable discharge in 1966," writes SF Jaye. "At that time, the Vietnam War was in full prominence; the world was getting ready for hippies; the Beatles and Stones dominated rock. I was searching for meaning. An idealistic youth."

"I was introduced to marijuana in 1966. No big deal," he continues. "In 1967, the hippies in Haight-Ashbury in San Francisco received a great deal of press from *Life* magazine, *Time, The Saturday Evening Post,* etc. Early in 1968, I was introduced to 'other drugs'. LSD, speed, hash, etc. I liked them and used them but didn't allow them to rule me."

In 1971, SF Jaye entered college and began studying hard. Three years later, his father died and he decided to give up drugs. "I continued my education, earned a Masters Degree in

Education Administration, joined a church, and became very involved in education and religion for the next 20 to 25 years. In 1978, I married my wife, Karen, to whom I am still married. From 1974 until 1995, I never smoked a cigarette, never drank liquor, never used drugs, and led a totally clean life, abstaining from drugs, crime, sin, and other activities."

In 1980, he developed a close friendship with a man named David. In the mid-1990s, David began taking methamphetamine—for reasons that are still unclear. Eventually, David offered meth to his friend, who was experiencing career and family problems at the time. SF was ripe for a diversion.

"I was a fitness enthusiast and spent a good deal of time working out," he says. "So when [David] offered something that would help increase my physical stamina and help eliminate depression, it seemed like it might be a good idea. So, I did a line. A few days later, another line. And that's about all it takes. A year later, I was using daily. Two years later, I was injecting it a couple times a day."

SF was working as a teacher at the time. "I was VERY, VERY careful to conceal my usage from everyone," he writes. "I kept my job through the whole thing and was never caught or suspected." His wife eventually discovered his drug secret. To prevent more marital discord, SF tried to kick his habit.

"She and I would throw [my drugs] away, destroy the needles, etc," SF writes. "Time and time again. But I'd go back to it. I wanted so badly to quit. But it was impossible. I continued to use at a maintenance level. This way, I could go to work and earn enough money to keep paying the mortgage, bills, and buy dope." In June 2001, SF lost his job—"for a reason totally unrelated to drug use," he insists. He informed a marriage counselor that he was a methamphetamine addict, then entered treatment.

"I quit using September 14, 2001," he writes. "I am now in an intensive outpatient program.

I go to therapy every day, individual counseling on a weekly basis and medical psychiatric counseling every other week. Meth addiction is very difficult to control and nearly impossible to stop."

SF graduated from his rehabilitation program on July 10, 2002. His web site doesn't offer any recent updates on his condition.

* * *

Missy, age 28, grew up between Red Wing, Minnesota, and Maiden Rock, Wisconsin. "My parents divorced when I was 15. My father was an alcoholic and very abusive, physically, verbally and sexually," recalls Missy. "My mom is and was a nurse who worked very hard but turned her back on the abuse my father dished out."

Missy's mother and father were laissez-faire about other things as well. "My parents were not very strict," she says. "They took us to the bar with them all the time, sometimes until 2 a.m., even on school nights. Sometimes, they tried to be strict but they were not consistent with it."

"I started smoking when I was 12 because my friends smoked. I began smoking in front of my parents when I was 14," she continues. "My parents let my sister and I start drinking in bars with them when I was 13 and my sister was 15. I smoked pot for the first time when I was 17, with a friend. I tried crank for the first time on New Year's Eve, 1996. I was at a house with some people and didn't want to sound stupid, so I told them that I had done it before. I tried my first line that night and started using it on weekends."

"My first experience with meth was scary," Missy admits. "I was scared of what it would do to me. I was scared of the effects. I also felt incredibly guilty because I had a four-month-old son ... but it also felt incredible. I felt focused, I felt energized, I felt superhuman and I felt efficient." A binge user, Missy would use meth nonstop, for 10 or 11 days at a time. The longest she ever stayed up was 27 days. "I was a complete zombie and passed out after smoking a gram. It couldn't keep me up anymore," she recalls.

The lowest point of Missy's addiction came on May 4, 2004, when she committed a burglary to feed her habit. "I broke into a local business half an hour before I knew the first person came to work," she says. "I broke into it through a window at 8:30 a.m., took all the money, ordered my drugs from my hook-up, and waited."

This experience shocked her back into a semblance of reality. "That afternoon, I was able to see what I had done to my life," she recalls. "I saw my addiction for the first time and wanted to die. I called my mom and told her everything about the drugs. I told her that I had about $1,300 written out of her checking account she didn't know about yet. I told her I wanted to die. I begged her to still love me and not turn her back on me."

"I went to treatment a week later," Missy continues. "But the night before I went, I told [my mother] that if she did not buy me some [meth], I would not go, and I would take my son, and she would never see us again. I made my mom pay for my drugs and I did them in front of her for the first time ever. I felt like she owed me, because I was going to detox the next day."

Drug rehabilitation was not an immediate success; within a week of going through treatment, Missy was back on speed. A second round of treatment ensued, this one more successful than the first. By the time she was interviewed, Missy said she was "almost three months clean."

"Quitting meth was the hardest thing I've ever done," she says. "I had no coping skills for problems. I had lost the ability to be happy. All I feel right now is dark and miserable. I have a hard time fathoming the thought of living life without ever getting f— up again."

* * *

Preventing others from going down the road to addiction became David Parnell's new goal once he recovered from surgery and rehabilitation. Parnell decided to fulfill his earlier, handwritten promise to his wife: he would devote himself to spreading the bad news about meth. He gave a testimonial at his church, spoke at several jails, and visited a school at a policeman's behest. These initial public appearances proved successful, and Parnell soon found himself in demand as a speaker. "I feel by being honest, I could help some people," says Parnell.

Around the same time he started giving lectures, Parnell also began doing interviews with the media. This exposure dramatically raised his profile, and soon he was fielding calls from around the world. People contacted him wanting to talk about their addiction to meth, or about a loved one who was hooked on the drug. Other people sent him letters begging for help.

Parnell's advice was both simple and powerful. He told people not to give up hope and to have faith in a higher power. He pointed to himself as an example of someone who successfully managed to kick meth, albeit at a steep price. "I tell young people to tell God to take it away," says Parnell of meth cravings.

For all his newfound spirituality, Parnell retains a level-headed perspective about his ability to help. "There's nothing I can say to change a kid, unless they are ready themselves," he says. "If [an addicted child] doesn't want to change, there's nothing I can do."

In 2004, Parnell reached out into cyberspace with the launch of his web site, *www.facingthedragon.org*. The site has testimonials from Parnell and other users, basic information on methamphetamine, and an explanation of 'tweaking': "A tweaker can appear normal: eyes can be clear, speech concise and movements brisk. But a closer look will reveal the person's eyes are moving ten times faster than normal, the voice has a slight quiver and movements are quick and jerky."

Parnell's professional life is currently given over to lectures, interviews, and his web site. In the first six months of 2005, Parnell spoke at about 80 schools. Parnell's web site lists his current occupation as motivational speaker. He spends his spare time with Amy and his seven children. He still lives in Tennessee and wants to put together a book about his life.

* * *

Parnell isn't the only former addict to evangelize about recovery on the Internet. After going through a grueling solo withdrawal while living in her Chevy Cavalier, Rashelle Chaplin started searching the web for meth support groups. She had difficulty locating any, so in the late 1990s, Chaplin decided to design her own online support site.

"I had no prior knowledge of web sites ... but determination works wonders," says Chaplin, who currently lives near St. Louis, Missouri.

"I taught myself [how to design sites], got the programs I needed, and bought what I needed to get something up and running." Chaplin adopted the name "Sky" as the nickname she uses on her web-boards. The tag is a shortened version of "skyzthelimit".

Located at *www.methmadness.com*, Chaplin's site offers gruesome imagery and stark text. Pictures of bone-thin women (meant to represent meth addicts) jostle for space with despairing tales of addiction. A flash/sound version of these pages comes complete with creepy music and sound effects. The site has a gothic feel to it, more akin to a horror movie than a recovery board. "My goal was to save one person from this horrible life," says Chaplin. "I have successfully saved lives of people who are now my close personal friends in real life, not just at my board."

Unlike Parnell, Chaplin/Sky takes a decidedly secular approach to reaching fellow addicts. "My goal with my board is to continue to

give unconditional, non-religious based support (which does work)," she explains, adding
that many addicts do not like having religion
shoved down their throats as a condition of
recovery.

Evidently, it's an approach that resonates
with people; Chaplin's web site is replete with
polls, poetry, and personal journals from various contributors. There's also an extensive pho-
to gallery of meth users past and present. With
the odd exception, the people featured in the
photographs look very ordinary. The pictures
look more like Employee of the Month shots
than portraits of hard-drug addicts.

When not moderating online chats and
touching up her site, Chaplin works as a professional commercial driver/trainer for the state of
Missouri. She serves as a Missouri state professional foster mother as well, which means she
has children in and out of her house all the time.
"I have no children via natural birth," she says.
"I did adopt an African-American crack baby

abandoned at birth. My own natural child was killed back in 1990, [by] a semi-truck driver on speed, of all things, that hit me head-on. I've had nine kids in my home that I've parented, one child adopted. Three kids are currently living with me."

She is divorced from her husband and no longer socializes with anyone from her addict days.

* * *

Not every meth-related Internet site is about recovery. The site *http://scotty-simmons.memory-of.com* features a memorial to William Scott Simmons, "born in Van Nuys, California on October 22, 1957 and passed away in Santa Cruz, California on October 16, 2004."

What follows is a detailed account of Simmons' descent into meth addiction, written by his former wife, Sherry. The site explains how the two met (in a bar in 1986), how they started taking meth together, how they fought like crazy, drifted apart, reunited, had children, had problems, and eventually separated. It also details Simmons' massive consumption of alcohol and drugs, the way he died (septic shock, following a round of necrotizing fasciitis), and the family he left behind.

"This is what our relationship was like," writes Simmons' spouse. "He would drink and use [methamphetamine] and I would yell and scream and accuse him of being on dope ... he would lie ... I would find his bag and bust him ... he would get pissed and leave or feel guilty and apologize ... This is the dance we did. He would leave ... I would hunt him down via phone or with my car. We would fight, make love, make up, and do it all over again."

"I left Scott [on] November 14th of 1994. I hoped it would be a wake-up call for him ... like a big smack in the head, but it wasn't. He spiraled down even further," Sherry says. "I would go see him from time to time or have him over for dinner (he usually didn't eat). I was having a hard time letting completely go of him. He would come to me every now and then and tell me he needed help and I would try to help him. He went in and out of drug rehab, Christian men's homes, but always returned to drugs."

Another online memorial can be found at *www.freewebs.com/kennysims*. The home page contains two illustrations of Jesus and a grim story about a young meth addict named Kenneth (Kenny) Glen Sims.

Written by Sims's elder sister, the site details his downward spiral into meth. Photos of Sims show a handsome, dark-haired young man, who gradually becomes more unkempt, thin, and wired-looking as the pictures near the end of his short life.

"Kenny was born February 10, 1980, to Walter and Janie Sims in Dallas, Texas," reads the introduction. "He had everything a child could want or need. Loving parents, a home, food and anything else you could imagine. Everyone was excited that the family now had someone to carry on the Sims name." As a child, Sims enjoyed baseball, football, and dressing up in his father's old Marine Corps camouflage outfit and playing war with his friends.

"At some point, he began smoking marijuana, which he was busted at school for and had to attend meetings and alternative school for punishment," writes Sims' sister. "Around 16 years old, he began smoking meth, which was introduced to him by an older man his girlfriend babysat for. He continued in this manner while his grades in school starting dropping and his interest in sports and other activities also started diminishing. He graduated from high school after attending summer school."

Sims moved out at age 20 and set up house with a girlfriend. He joined an electrical union and attended school to become an electrician. He bought a car —a Chevy S10—and appeared to be doing well. "We were all excited for him, because it seemed his life was turning in the right direction and things were looking good. Then a friend of his, from the electrical union, taught him how to shoot up speed (meth)," writes his sister.

His life went quickly downhill: Sims lost his job, apartment, and girlfriend. He spent a couple years shooting speed and hung out with assorted miscreants. He died on September 24, 2002 at the age of 22.

Sims's family came home one day to discover a police detective had left a message on their answering machine, asking Kenny's parents to call him. "Mom called the number. [When] they answered 'Homicide' and [asked], 'What is the victim's name?' she knew right away," writes Sims's sister. The family was told that Kenny was found on a back porch, unconscious and barely breathing. He died of a meth overdose.

CHAPTER 5

Stamping Out Meth Addiction

Shortly after the turn of the millennium, Doug Pamenter began to notice an alarming trend among his clients. An addictions counselor at a center for young offenders in Edmonton, Alberta, Pamenter observed that a growing number of teenagers were taking methamphetamine. Disturbed, Pamenter alerted his superiors, who seemed unconcerned. They felt that meth, like amphetamine in the 1960s, would eventually fall out of fashion. Pamenter wasn't so sure—crank was having "horrendous aftereffects" on his clients, he recalls. Indeed, as Pamenter was soon to discover, today's meth has little in common with the drug peddled in the 1960s. It's considerably stronger and it's also a lot more widely available. Users don't have to be friends with bikers to buy meth anymore.

Pamenter began researching methamphetamine, digging up as much information as he could about the drug. He spoke with police and psychologists who had first-hand experience dealing with meth. He also discovered the *www. kci.org* web site, which provided a wealth of meth-related information. Inspired, Pamenter launched his own site, *www.crystalrecovery. com*. Working in partnership with *www.kci.org* and with a handful of volunteers, the site gradually filled out. A long-time meth user known as "Lisa" was instrumental in adding content.

For a variety of reasons, Pamenter's web site was not popular with his bosses. They felt the site was a conflict of interest, since he was working in a young offenders center. Pamenter eventually quit his job in Alberta, and moved farther west to British Columbia. He currently teaches the Addiction Worker/Addiction Counselor program at CDI College in Abbotsford, B.C.

The site *www.crystalrecovery.com* is similar to David Parnell and Rashelle Chaplin's sites, except that a non-user with a counseling background put it together. It's more far-ranging and comprehensive as well. The site contains fact sheets, confessions, essays about addicted members, and several truly depressing letters. ("Hey. I'm 15 and I've been using meth for nine months. I'm addicted. I've been sober for about three weeks now, but not by choice. And it's been hell for me.) It also includes a very active chat room and message board. (One posting's title reads: "I'm glad my son is in jail."). Visitors to the web site will also find some disturbing artwork by addicts.

The site is intended to convey a simple

TIPS FOR QUITTING METH

1. Set small goals that are easier to reach. Be realistic about what you can achieve.
2. Get rid of your drugs and drug paraphernalia.
3. Throw out phone numbers that trigger thoughts about using.
4. Become aware of your using patterns.
5. Avoid any thing, any place, or anyone that might trigger you to use.
6. Schedule your day thoroughly. Boredom is ENEMY #1 for most crystal users.
7. Anticipate withdrawal.
8. Make a plan.
9. Watch your eating habits. Limit your intake of caffeine, sugar, and white flour products.
10. Try alternative therapies to ease withdrawal.
11. Get a health check-up.
12. Exercise.
13. Get support. Don't do it alone!
14. Be patient. Rome wasn't built in a day.
15. Explore your treatment options.

message: don't mess with meth. It offers tips to get off the drug, and links where people can seek help. For those thinking about experimenting with meth, the site offers disgusting photographs of meth cookers scorched in fires of their own making or scalded by chemical spills. If that weren't enough, Pamenter's site also boasts a horrifying collection of "before and after" shots of hard-core meth addicts. Most of the latter start off relatively clean-cut and end up skinny, scabby, and strung out.

A do-it-yourself project, Pamenter pays for site upkeep out of his own pocket although donations are welcome. Run on a shoestring, *www.crystalrecovery.com* isn't connected to a treatment facility or government agency—which is all too typical. As the National Association of Counties (NACo) noted in their meth survey, "The growth of the use and addiction to methamphetamines has occurred so fast and to such a degree that many local governments are scrambling to catch up."

The federal governments of both Canada and the United States are also struggling to get a handle on meth. Members of the U.S. Congress, for example, formed a "Meth Caucus" in 2000 to shed light on the issue. Originally founded by four Congressmen, the Caucus now boasts 100 members from both the Republican and Democrat sides of the House.

"Our goal is to educate Members of Congress, their staff and the American public about the growing lethal threat that meth abuse and production poses to all facets of our communities," writes Congressman Ken Calvert, co-chair of the Caucus, on their web page (*www.house. gov/larsen/meth*).

However, it doesn't appear that the Meth Caucus' message has reached the White House Office of National Drug Control Policy (ONDCP). As one of the biggest players in the federal anti-drug scene, ONDCP reps have voiced a few concerns about meth. Despite this, the ONDCP still seems clueless about how to deal with the drug. The organization's much touted web site, *www.theantidrug.com*, for example, contains a drop of information on methamphetamine in an ocean of data on marijuana. Likewise, the

ONDCP's television ads are still primarily about cannabis, not speed.

Individuals such as Pamenter, and organizations, such as Crystal Meth Anonymous (CMA), are trying to fill in the gaps when it comes to public awareness about methamphetamine. Founded in Los Angeles in 1993, Crystal Meth Anonymous is closely modeled after Alcoholic Anonymous. The group currently runs 150 chapters in the United States, Canada, New Zealand, and elsewhere. Will H., outgoing chairman of CMA World Services, describes the organization as "a spiritually based 12-step program offering the support of one crystal meth addict helping another to recovery from addiction to crystal meth." He goes on to say, "As an organization, we don't speculate on the medical aspects of our addictions. We merely offer peer-to-peer support in staying clean."

Members "include peoples of all races, income levels, educational backgrounds, sexes and sexually orientation," he says. "In the early years of the fellowship, the majority of the members were gay men, but that has changed over time. Our membership now includes a very wide cross-section of the U.S. population."

Like *www.crystalrecovery.com*, CMA operates on a tiny budget. Scant funds don't limit the group's effectiveness, however. David M., for example, credits CMA with saving his life. "What is the best aspect of Crystal Meth Anonymous?" he asks. "What I'd like everyone to know is that there is hope. We don't have to die anymore; the program works if you use it."

"The rooms of CMA are filled with men who loved me before I could love myself," adds David. "They may not have known me personally, but they in some way shared my experience. They knew where I'd come from and what I was going through and what I could be if I just stuck with it and worked the steps."

Aside from CMA, there are few support groups specifically geared towards meth. While *www.crystalrecovery.com* and *www.methmadness.com* provide a cyberspace presence, they aren't much help to people who don't have a computer. NACo noted the lack of bricks and mortar treatment services for meth users in their survey. The vast majority of law officers who responded to the survey reported that their county lacked "a meth rehabilitation center or program."

Because of this, "many meth abusers of this drug who have committed crimes are housed in local jails," states the report. Prison, however, is a lousy option. Such institutions are usually rampant with underground drug dealing. Put a meth addict in such an environment and it's a safe bet they'll buy drugs from an inmate rather than go through the pain of withdrawal. Meth users who inject in prison run the risk of contracting blood-borne HIV or Hepatitis C from sharing dirty needles (since syringes are in short supply in prisons).

While rehab would seem like a better alternative than remand, no one is sure of the best way to treat meth addiction. "There are no specific, well-established treatments for dependence on amphetamine or amphetamine-like drugs and few controlled studies on the treatment of amphetamine dependence," reads a paper written by Dr. Richard Rawson of the Matrix Institute (a non-profit organization that treats substance abuse), along with Dr. Walter Ling and Dr. Jerome Jaffe.

The lack of a methadone-type drug is one of the biggest stumbling blocks in treating crank addicts. Despite the similarity of names, methadone is completely different from methamphetamine. Invented during World War II, methadone is a synthetic opiate that can ease heroin users through withdrawal. Like a nicotine patch, methadone takes away cravings but doesn't make the user high. Nothing like methadone exists for speed. "There is currently no medication that can quickly and safely help reverse the effects of overdoses or help reduce withdrawal, paranoia and psychotic symptoms associated with methamphetamine use," notes the Canadian Center on Substance Abuse in Ottawa.

Researchers in Europe have toyed with the idea of giving methamphetamine addicts legal access to their drug of choice. The hope is that by prescribing pharmaceutical grade methamphetamine, users would be less likely to overdose (since overdose cases are often caused by impure black market product), share needles, or take drugs in public. While heroin prescription is an established practice in parts of Europe, little is known about the efficacy of prescribing meth. Few studies have been conducted on the subject. Even if the approach is valid, meth prescription is unlikely to make an appearance in North America any time soon. Most U.S. and Canadian drug policy and treatment experts would rather focus on rehabilitation.

Some officials, however, question whether there's even any point in trying to treat meth users. They maintain that meth is so addictive

that it's futile to put addicts into expensive rehabilitation programs. According to a commonly
cited statistic, only five percent of meth addicts
are able to successfully give up the drug.

Dr. Robert Perkinson, clinical director
of the Keystone Treatment Center in Canton,
South Dakota, takes the opposite tack. Keystone
treats addicts of all stripes, whether their problems are alcohol-, drug-, or gambling-related.
Dr. Perkinson believes it is possible to beat a
meth habit, although the process is neither fast
nor easy. "Meth addiction is best treated with a
long inpatient stay, plus five years of follow-up,"
says Dr. Perkinson. "[Ninety percent] of patients
that work our program stay clean and sober,"
Dr. Perkinson writes on the Keystone web site
(*www.keystonetreatment.com*).

Located on a 30-acre spread in a rural setting, Keystone has been offering treatment
services for roughly three decades. According
to Dr. Perkinson, the gender split among meth
patients at Keystone is 60 percent male, 40

percent female. The center provides around-the-clock nursing care and boasts a staff that includes psychiatrists, psychologists, chemical dependency counselors, family counselors, a full-time teacher, and religious clergy of all denominations. Keystone programs are based on a 12-step model.

Keystone is experimenting to see whether there are any medications that can aid meth treatment. To this end, Keystone uses tranquilizers, such as Ativan and Valium, as well as anti-psychotic drugs, such as Thorazine and Seroquel, to help addicts cope with withdrawal. Other facilities have experimented with Prozac and other substances, with mixed results.

Like Keystone, the Matrix Institute of Los Angeles offers help for a wide variety of drug and alcohol addictions. A non-profit organization founded in 1984, the Matrix Institute conducts research, training, and treatment. Meth users are part of the overall patient mix.

The average meth patient at the Matrix

is "lower income white or Hispanic, and 32 years old," says Dr. Rawson. Clients are evenly split between men and women, and their preferred method of injesting meth is "60 percent smoke, 25 percent inject, 15 percent snort."

Only half of the Matrix's meth patients are there voluntarily. The rest arrived as a term of sentencing from drug court, or courtesy of Proposition 36 (a groundbreaking "citizen's initiative" passed by California voters in 2000, under which low-level drug offenders are sent to treatment rather than jail).

As one of a handful of meth experts in the United States, Dr. Rawson and other Matrix staff created a manual on treating amphetamine or methamphetamine addicts on an outpatient basis. Published in the 1980s, funding for the manual came from the National Institute on Drug Abuse (NIDA). The methods cited in the manual became known as the "Matrix Model," or more simply, the "Matrix approach."

"The Matrix approach evolved over time,

incorporating treatment elements with support from scientific evidence, including cognitive behavioral therapies (i.e., relapse prevention techniques), a positive reinforcing treatment context, many components of motivational interviewing, family involvement, accurate psychoeducational information, 12-step facilitation efforts and regular urine testing," writes Dr. Rawson and Rachel Gonzales, in an unpublished manuscript.

"The approach is delivered using a combination of group and individual sessions delivered approximately three times per week over a 16-week period followed by a 36-week continuing care support group and 12-step program participation," continue the authors. "Over 15,000 cocaine and methamphetamine users have been treated with this approach during the past 20 years."

In 1999, the Center for Substance Abuse Treatment (CSAT) funded a research project to test the effectiveness of the Matrix Model.

"Roughly 1,000 methamphetamine dependent individuals were admitted into eight different treatment study sites," reads Dr. Rawson and Gonzales's account. "In each of the eight sites, 50% of the participants were assigned to either Matrix treatment or to a 'treatment as usual' (TAU) condition, which comprised a variety of counseling techniques idiosyncratic to each site.

"The study result showed that individuals assigned to treatment in the Matrix approach received substantially more treatment services, were retained in treatment longer, gave more methamphetamine negative urine samples during treatment and completed treatment at a higher rate than those in the TAU condition," they continue. "These in treatment data suggested a superior response to the Matrix approach."

That said, research outcomes proved very similar between the two groups. "Follow-up data indicated that over 60 percent of both treatment groups reported no methamphetamine use and gave urine samples that tested negative for methamphetamine (and cocaine) use," state Dr. Rawson and Gonzales. "Use of other drugs, such as alcohol and marijuana, were also significantly reduced."

In other words, while the Matrix Model might not be any better than other rehabilitation methods, meth treatment works. Researchers hope such studies will convince the feds to put more money into meth treatment and prevention. Dr. Rawson is not entirely optimistic about this possibility, however. When asked to describe a best and worst case scenario for the future, Dr. Rawson sent the following reply via email:

"Best case scenario: Congressmen put pressure on the White House to respond. They put money into prevention, education, treatment, training and research. Drug courts expanded dramatically. Over time, meth becomes stigmatized the way crack cocaine became stigmatized in the early 1990s. Meth becomes a nasty loser's drug. Kids view it as very uncool. We get more treatments that work, including medications. Replacement medications eliminate the use of pseudoephedrine, so home labs become non-existent. International efforts limit the amount of bulk ephedrine and pseudoephedrine floating around the international market unaccounted for. Still will be some available and will maintain a low level of use in some rural and suburban areas.

"Worst-case scenario: War and Hurricane Katrina, deficit, etc. No money for anything, including cops. Meth production in home labs and Mexican labs and other bulk producers around the world increases. Use in raves and clubs increases, meth becomes more trendy, use with gays continues at high levels, increasing HIV transmission, injection route of administration increases and Hepatitis and HIV increase in heterosexual community. No prevention efforts around high risk sex and meth, Hep[atitis]

C/HIV/AIDS and we start seeing increase in heterosexual activity. More myths about meth users not responding to treatment spreads, use continues and expands into cities and the African-American community and becomes an endemic problem."

Back on Canada's west coast, Pamenter has equally strong opinions on what governments in Canada and the United States should be doing. "I think education and prevention are the answer," he says. "Take away the demand and you do not need to worry about the supply. Every dollar spent on prevention saves six to seven dollars later on treatment costs. [Government should put] more money for treatment, too."

Former users such as Dave Parnell don't have a lot to say about government drug policy, other than hard-line measures targeting addicts aren't likely to work. "A lot of the times, the cops want to lock up everyone and throw away the key," says Parnell. "But you can't lock up everyone."

As for himself, Parnell says a peaceful home life is key to maintaining a sober existence.

"I've got my kids back and I live in a healing environment," he says.

A Timeline of Methamphetamine

1887 Amphetamine is synthesized in a German lab. Scientists are unsure what to do with it.

1919 Methamphetamine is synthesized in a Japanese lab. Scientists are still unsure what to do with the substance.

1920s–1930s
Pharmaceutical companies begin to take interest in the new drug when it's discovered that amphetamine helps clear blocked up nasal and bronchial passages.

1932 The Smith, Kline & French pharmaceutical firm markets amphetamine as a decongestant and sells it under the brand name "Benzedrine." The product is packaged as an over-the-counter inhaler.

1930s Amphetamine is found to have an oddly calming effect on hyperactive children. It is also discovered that amphetamine helps people suffering from narcolepsy (a rare disease that causes people to repeatedly fall asleep).

1930s There's increasing awareness of amphetamine's ability to energize users and ward off sleep.

World War II (1939–1945)
Soldiers on both sides of the conflict are given huge doses of amphetamine and methamphetamine to bolster courage and help them fight all night. Hitler himself is rumored to be a regular user of meth.

1940 Burroughs Wellcome pharmaceutical company markets methamphetamine under the brand name "Methedrine."

Korean War (1950–1953)
American troops receive amphetamines before heading into battle.

1950s Post-war amphetamine epidemic occurs in Japan. Addiction becomes common as workers pop "pep pills" to rebuild their shattered country following World War II.

1950s In spite of growing public awareness of the dangerous, addictive qualities of amphetamine and methamphetamine, the drug still finds new uses as a diet aid and anti-depressant.

Early 1960s
While the Beatles rely on amphetamine pills to stay on their feet during all night concerts in Hamburg, Germany, President John F. Kennedy uses several drugs, including amphetamines, in the management of various ailments.

1965 Amendments to the U.S. Food and Drug Act criminalize most non-medical use and manufacture of amphetamine and methamphetamine.

1960s A black market emerges in amphetamine and methamphetamine. Outlaw bike gangs largely handle illegal manufacture and distribution of meth.

Late 1960s
Amphetamine/methamphetamine gets a bad reputation, even in the burgeoning drug culture of the era. The expression "Speed Kills" enters the common lexicon. Users of meth are derided as "speed freaks."

1969 America's first methamphetamine lab bust happens in Santa Cruz, California.

1970 U.S. Congress passes the Comprehensive Drug Abuse Prevention and Control Act. The Act places illicit substances into "schedules" according to their perceived level of harm. Meth eventually ends up in "Schedule II"—a category for drugs with medical uses but a high potential for abuse. The only way to buy meth legally is with a doctor's prescription.

1970s   Underground use of meth continues on a small scale. Use is limited to a few West Coast cities such as San Diego.

1980s   Discovery that ephedrine can be used as a precursor substance for meth. Ephedrine-based meth recipes proliferate.

Late 1980s

After the U.S. federal government cracks down on ephedrine, meth cookers switch to pseudoephedrine (a product found in many cold and sinus medications).

Mid-1990s
Advent of the Internet proves a huge boon for methamphetamine makers. Highly guarded meth recipes become available online for anyone to download.

Mid-1990s
Mexican organized crime gangs muscle aside bike gangs to take over the meth trade. Emergence of "super labs" allow huge amounts of meth to be churned out at a time.

Mid-1990s
Methamphetamine use soars in the United States.

2004 National Conference of State Legislatures issues a briefing paper that describes meth as "the fastest growing drug threat in America."

2005 A survey by the National Association of Counties (NACo) reveals most local law enforcement officers view

methamphetamine as their biggest drug problem.

2005 *Newsweek* magazine runs a cover story on meth, "America's Most Dangerous Drug," August 8, 2005.

2005 U.S. Federal Government concedes to the dangers of meth. U.S. Attorney General Alberto Gonzales is quoted as saying, "In terms of damage to children and to our society, meth is now the most dangerous drug in America."

Amazing Facts and Figures

- By the end of 1971, at least 31 amphetamine preparations (including amphetamine-sedative, amphetamine-tranquilizer, and amphetamine-analgesic combinations) were legally distributed by 15 pharmaceutical companies.

- An estimated 26 million people worldwide used methamphetamine, amphetamine, or related substances in 2003. Almost two-thirds of the world's amphetamine and methamphetamine users live in East and Southeast Asia.

- In 2004, an estimated 12 million people in the United States (4.9 percent of the U.S. population age 12 or older) had used methamphetamine at least once in their lifetime; 1.4 million (0.5 percent) had used it in the past year, and 600,000 (0.2 percent) had used it in the past month.

- The Canadian Addiction Survey (2004) reported that 6.4 percent of respondents aged 15 and older have used amphetamines at least once. Less than 1 percent reported past-year use.

WHAT TO DO IF YOU ENCOUNTER A CLANDESTINE METH LAB

DO NOT touch anything in the lab

DO NOT turn on or off power switches or lights

DO NOT eat or drink in or around the lab

DO NOT open or move chemicals or suspected chemicals

DO NOT smoke anywhere near the lab

DO NOT sniff any containers

DO decontaminate yourself and your clothes

DO wash your hands and face thoroughly

DO call the authorities

Source: Drug Enforcement Administration website, www.usdoj.gov/dea/concern/methlab_whattodo.html

- In the first six months of 2004, nearly 59 percent of substance abuse treatment admissions (excluding alcohol) in Hawaii, were for primary methamphetamine abuse. San Diego followed, with nearly 51 percent. Notable increases in methamphetamine treatment admissions occurred in Atlanta (10.6 percent in the first six months of 2004, as compared with 2.5 percent in 2001) and Minneapolis/St. Paul (18.7 percent in the first six months of 2004, as compared with 10.6 percent in 2001).

- Meth lab operations have been uncovered in all 50 U.S. states; Missouri tops the list, with more than 8000 labs, equipment caches, and toxic dumps seized between 2002 and 2004.

- A Center for Disease Control and Prevention study on hazardous substance-release events found that methamphetamine labs caused injury to 79 first-responders (police officers, firefighters, EMTs, and hospital personnel) in 14 states participating in the study. The most common injuries were respiratory and eye irritation, headache, dizziness, nausea and vomiting, and shortness of breath. In addition to the dangerous nature of methamphetamine production, the labs are often booby-trapped and workers are well armed.

METHAMPHETAMINE STREET PRICES 2003

	POUND	OUNCE	GRAM
POWDER	$1,600-$45,000	$270-$5,000	$20-$300
ICE	$6,000-$70,000	$500-$3,100	$60-$700

Source: Drug Enforcement Administration, "National Drug Threat Assessment 2005"

- The DEA spends an estimated $145 million annually to combat methamphetamine. This includes $119 million on enforcement, tracking chemicals, and investigating illegal shipments of pseudoephedrine, ephedrine, and other precursors used to manufacture methamphetamine. It also includes approximately $4 million in DEA funds for lab cleanup and almost $2 million for lab cleanup equipment. In addition, the DEA manages $20 million from the Community Oriented Police Services (COPS) program which is dispersed for state and local lab cleanup.

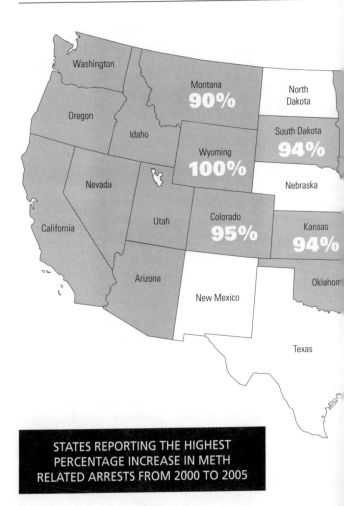

STATES REPORTING THE HIGHEST
PERCENTAGE INCREASE IN METH
RELATED ARRESTS FROM 2000 TO 2005

Source: "The Meth Epidemic in America" by the National Association of Counties, July 2005.

CRYSTAL METH FAST FACTS

TRUE OR FALSE?

99 PER CENT	5 PER CENT	5 YEARS
of first-time meth users are hooked after just the first try	of meth addicts are able to kick it and stay away	the life expectancy of a habitual meth user from the first hit to the last breath

All three "facts" are false—The first two have never been studied and would be very difficult if not impossible to determine. The third is false. These "statistics" are cited on a web site established by one American state's Attorney General's Office. The statements are widely cited around the United States and Canada as true statistics and have actually been used to argue against funding the apparently hopeless task of treating meth users.

Source: Dr. Richard Rawson and Rachel Gonzales, "Methamphetamine Addiction: Does Treatment Work?"

HOW CAN I FIGHT METH IN MY COMMUNITY?

- Contact your local law enforcement if you think there might be a meth lab in your neighborhood
- Start a neighborhood watch and look for signs of meth labs
- Talk to your children about methamphetamine
- Get involved with any community meth action teams your town may have and if there isn't a local group, start one
- If you have experience with methamphetamine, share that knowledge with others

Source: www.house.gov/larsen/meth/information.shtml

- In 2006, the provinces of Manitoba, Saskatchewan, and Alberta all decided to restrict the sale of cold remedies and other drugs that contain pseudoephedrine. Pharmacies across the Prairies must now sell these drugs from behind the counter. British Columbia is monitoring bulk sales of these drugs and is considering retail restrictions, while Yukon pharmacies are voluntarily moving them behind the counter.

- In British Columbia, Canada, the number of deaths related to methamphetamine rose from 3 in 2000 to 33 in 2004.

- The number of methamphetamine treatment admissions to publicly funded drug treatment facilities increased from 58,795 in 1999 to 66,975 in 2000, 81,799 in 2001, and 104,481 in 2002, representing 5.5 percent of all admissions. During 2002, of the admissions to treatment for methamphetamine/amphetamine, 55.4 percent were male and 74.3 percent were white.

- In 2002, epidemic abuse of amphetamine-type stimulants (ATS), particularly among school-aged youth, remained Thailand's most serious illegal drug problem.

- Women use methamphetamine at rates equal to men. Use of other major illicit drugs is characterized by ratios of 3:1 men to women (heroin) or 2:1 (cocaine). More than 70 percent of methamphetamine-dependent women report histories of physical and sexual abuse.

- Every pound (0.5 kg) of methamphetamine produces an average of five or six pounds (2.5 to 3 kg) of chemical waste.

What Others Say

"The first thing people on methamphet-amine lose is their common sense; suddenly, anything goes, including unprotected sex with many different partners in a single night— which is among the most efficient ways to spread HIV and other sexually transmitted diseases."

"Higher Risk", Michael Specter, The New Yorker, June 23, 2005

"Methamphetamine has a 9-to-12-hour half-life, which means that weekend war-riors can start on Thursday and only dose five times to make it to Sunday evening."

Steven Shoptaw, psychologist with the UCLA Integrated Substance Abuse Programs

"The use of stigmatizing terms, such as "ice babies" and "meth babies" lack scientific validity and should not be used. Experience with similar labels applied to children exposed parentally to cocaine demonstrates that such labels harm the children to which they are applied, lowering expectations for their academic and life achievements, discouraging investigation into other causes for physical and social problems the child might encounter."

Dr. David Lewis, Professor of Community Health and Medicine, Brown University

"What drunk drivers are to emergency rooms, meth is to a burn center."

Doctor quoted in, "Meth Lab Explosions Put Hospital Burn Units in a Bind" by Leon Alligood, The Tennessean, April 10, 2005

"Parents need to talk to their kids about meth ... Some of the most common signs and symptoms are extremely dilated pupils, dry or bleeding nose and lips, chronic nasal or sinus problems, and bad breath. Because meth is a stimulant, users also experience hyperactivity and irritability. This includes a lack of interest in sleep and food, leading to drastic weight loss or anorexia."

From www.theantidrug.com, web site sponsored by the Office of National Drug Control Policy

"I think it is fair to say that I'm the person responsible for making clandestine [meth] cooking what it is today—a burgeoning pastime."

Steve Presiler, quoted in "A Madness Called Meth." Special Report by the McClatchy Company of newspapers, California, October 8, 2000

"It's a terrible situation, especially when you consider that most meth patients are from rural America. These are good ol' boys who have become addicted to this stuff and it's absolutely destroyed their lives, and in rural areas there are fewer mental health and other services than you would find in a metropolitan area."

Social worker quoted in "Meth Lab Explosions Put Hospital Burn Units in a Bind" by Leon Alligood, The Tennessean, April 10, 2005

"Most of the danger in meth labs comes from accidents. The drug's ingredients are so volatile that explosions occur in the smallest labs ... as well as the finest assemblies of heating mantles ... A single pint of ether, for instance, can blow up a small home. One cooker made a mistake that ended with a blast that blew a house off its foundation."

"At Meth's Door" by Kevin Cook, August 1996, Details magazine

"More than any other controlled substance, methamphetamine trafficking endangers children through exposure to drug abuse, neglect, physical and sexual abuse, toxic chemicals, hazardous waste, fire, and explosions."

Testimony of Joseph Rannazzisi, deputy chief, Office of Enforcement Operations, Drug Enforcement Administration, before U.S. Congress, November 18, 2004

"I felt my face just melting. The skin was running down my arm ... like lard."

Ricky Dale Houchens, Kentucky, talking about a meth-lab explosion in a trailer, Newsweek magazine, August 8, 2005

"Since many meth ingredients are flammable, one false move by a cook can yield disaster. When Selena Humphrey, 19, used to make the drug with her friends, "we were always on pins and needles," she says, as they would accidentally spill chemicals or start small fires. Eventually, an explosion sent her to Vanderbilt [Hospital burn unit] where doctors had to chisel melted plastic—which had lined the walls of the lab—off her face."

"America's Most Dangerous Drug," Newsweek magazine cover story, August 8, 2005,

"Crystal meth does not discriminate; it preys on white-collar professionals, students, the working class, the skid row bum, and everybody in between."

"Fast Facts About Crystal Meth," www.crystalrecovery.com web site

"Crystal meth is the first 'gender equal' drug, with equal numbers of male and female users."

"Fast Facts About Crystal Meth", www.crystalrecovery.com web site

"... The methamphetamine threat cannot be defeated without better control of precursor chemicals, like ephedrine and pseudoephedrine, which are used to make the drug. Chemical diversion exists at the retail, wholesale, and international levels, requiring a comprehensive plan to stop diversion at each of these levels."

U.S. Attorney General Alberto Gonzales, quoted in press release, Office of National Drug Control Policy, May 23, 2005

"For the most part, the allure and abundance of methamphetamine can be attributed to its convenience. Like fast-food chains, methamphetamine is widely available and inexpensive to purchase."

Dr. Richard Rawson and Rachel Gonzales, in an unpublished manuscript, "Methamphetamine Addiction: Does Treatment Work?"

"It looks like you told the person to stand up and took a sledgehammer to their mouth, the destruction is so complete,"
Dr. Jeffrey Paskar, a Springfield, Missouri, dentist

"The white, trailer-trash guy with tattoos and a t-shirt, drinking beer, chain-smoking and shooting speed with dirty kids crawling around being neglected is the poster child [for methamphetamine abuse] ... But there are a lot of different use patterns out there. There is the middle-class white woman who gets it from a psychiatrist's prescription, there are people who binge as a couple every few months, there are students who use it to study. So how representative is the stereotypical speed freak? I don't think anyone knows."

Craig Reinarman, professor of sociology at the University of California at Santa Cruz.

"Meth is a real problem for some people, but it is an over-hyped problem. All you have to do is look at the use rates and look at sentencing. When 100,000 people a year die from alcohol, I'm still saying that's the most dangerous drug in America."

Jason Zeidenberg, executive director of the Justice Policy Institute, in "The Methamphetamine Epidemic—Less Than Meets the Eye", published 2005 by the Drug Reform Coordination Network

"My name is Jennifer, and I am 24 years old and I was widowed at the age of 22. My husband's name was Tony, he was 30 years old and he died of acute methamphetamine overdose, on April 22, 2003."

Letter published on www.crystalrecovery.com

"Compared to opiate withdrawal (heroin, etc), meth withdrawal is physically fairly mild. The primary withdrawal symptoms are emotional. Poor judgment, mood swings, and emotional volatility may continue for several months in early recovery."

Will H., outgoing chairman of Crystal Meth Anonymous World Services

"Meth is not like other drugs that are refinements of naturally occurring chemicals, such as cocaine or heroin. Meth is more of a poison than a drug. It is a poison that gets the user high. In this sense, meth is more like glue or gas—and who in their right mind would want to use those!"

Doug Pamenter, creator of www.crystalrecovery.com

"In my opinion [meth] is the most psychologically addictive (common) illegal drug. Meth is worse than cigarettes. Plus, there is significant physical addiction that takes place as is evidenced by the withdrawal symptoms of severe depression, fatigue, etc. The secondary psychological addiction is huge—which is the fear of coming down, or fear of withdrawal."

Doug Pamenter, www.crystalrecovery.com

"In central Missouri, nearly every case of child abuse involves meth. Social workers in Franklin County keep a log of parents under investigation and the circumstances involved; this spring, it read: Cocaine. Meth. Medical and physical neglect. Meth. Sexual abuse. Meth. Meth. Manufacturing meth."

Stephanie Simon, "Meth's Grip in Midwest Strangles Authorities", Los Angeles Times, June 27, 2005

"When you see penalties that would require life imprisonment, the same kind of penalty that you see for the trafficking of heroin, that has to send out a very significant signal."

Saskatchewan premier, Lorne Calvert, on proposals to increase meth penalties in Canada

"Eight long years of abusing this drug took its toll on me physically, emotionally, and mentally. The amazing thing is that I am still alive to tell my story. I am proud, not ashamed of allowing my story to be told, because I hope that others will see what I had to go through and understand that this drug ... is not the best medicine for life's problems ..."

Rashelle Chaplin, writing as "Sky" on her web site, www.methmadness.com)

"Most detox centers and treatment facilities are geared to dealing with depressants: alcohol, heroin, benzodiazepines; and are less able to deal with stimulants, such as cocaine and meth."

Doug Pamenter, creator of www.crystalrecovery.com

"We know that the vast majority of Americans who use cold medication and prescription drugs do so legitimately. We are working to maintain Americans' access to these medications but reduce the threat of their diversion and abuse."

John Walters, director of the Office of National Drug Control Policy

"I average about a 60–70% yield of clean pseudo. Not the greatest, but that's only because I am particularly lazy when it comes to following some of these steps."

Anonymous, downloaded from Internet article "Extracting Pseudoephedrine From Cold and Sinus Pills"

"Kids on crystal just lose it, break things, do property damage. They hurt themselves."

Youth shelter worker, quoted in "City Braces for Meth Explosion", Toronto Star, June 20, 2005

"Methamphetamine is undeniably a uniquely destructive drug."

Scott Burns, Deputy Director for State and Local Affairs, Office of National Drug Control Policy

"… Methamphetamine presents some unique challenges. First, it is synthetic, relying on no harvested crops for its manufacture. Unfortunately, the 'recipe' to manufacture this synthetic drug is relatively straightforward, and easy to find on the Internet … Second, meth has hit rural areas in the United States particularly hard, communities where resources to combat this drug are less available. Third, methamphetamine is a particularly intense stimulant, highly addictive, and overwhelmingly dangerous."

Joseph Rannazzisi, deputy chief, Office of Enforcement Operations, Drug Enforcement Administratio

"I think we would all agree that methamphetamine is the most destructive, dangerous, terrible drug that's come along in a long time."

Scott Burns, Deputy Director for State and Local Affairs, Office of National Drug Control Policy

"The bipartisan House Meth Caucus that I co-chair is designed to help Members of Congress coordinate our legislative and educational efforts to fight this deadly problem. By providing our colleagues with information about the ever-growing meth epidemic and offering policy solutions, we can help stop the scourge of meth before more lives are devastated. Our society, our neighborhoods and our children are at risk because of meth."

Congressman Chris Cannon, U.S. Congress House Meth Caucus

"Heroin is still considered by most professionals to be the drug that causes the most
damage [to addicts], however you wish to
interpret that; but meth, in my opinion,
causes far more long-term damage to a
user's brain and to a lesser degree, body."

Doug Pamenter, creator of
www.crystalrecovery.com

"It still seems that nicotine is the hardest
drug to quit because every puff of a cigarette is like an IV bolus of amphetamine.
The issue about permanent brain damage
is looking bad for methamphetamine addicts, but the body has a way of making
new brain cells or redirecting neuronal
connections. Most likely, we will find
that amphetamines permanently
damage the brain, but the brain
recovers much of what was lost.".

Dr. Robert Perkinson, clinical director
of the Keystone Treatment Center

"Canada's battle against crystal methamphetamine is just beginning, but the drug already has a firm foothold on the Prairies."

"Meth War Rages On" in the Winnipeg Sun, January 3, 2006

"The worst thing about it was that I was addicted the first time I did it. It drags you down that quick. That's probably the scariest thing."

A 21-year-old Saskatchewan woman currently suing her meth dealer, quoted in the Winnipeg Sun, January 3, 2006

Select Bibliography

Baum, Dan. *Smoke and Mirrors: The War on Drugs and the Politics of Failure.* New York: Little, Brown and Company, 1996.

Blackwell, Judith, and Patricia Erickson, eds. *Illicit Drugs in Canada.* Scarborough: Nelson Canada, 1988.

Brecher, Edward M., and the editors of *Consumer Reports* magazine. *The Consumers Union Report on Licit and Illicit Drugs.* New York: Little Brown & Co, 1973.

Strausbaugh, John, and Donald Blaise, eds. *The Drug User: Documents 1840–1960.* New York: Blast Books, 1990.

Interviews

B., Abby. Interview by the author.

Chaplin, Rashelle. Interview by the author.

H., Will. Interview by the author.

M., David. Interview by the author.

Missy. Interview by the author.

Murphy, Katie. Interview by the author.

Pamenter, Doug. Interview by the author.

Parnell, Dave. Interview by the author.

Perkinson, Dr. Robert. Interview by the author.

Rawson, Dr. Richard. Interview by the author.

Red [*pseud.*]. Interview by the author.

Web sites

www.drugwarfacts.org/methamph.htm

www.kci.org

www.crystalrecovery.com

www.methmadness.com

www.facingthedragon.org

www.drugabuse.gov/NIDA_Notes/NNVol11N5/Tearoff.html

www.theantidrug.com

www.crystalmeth.org
www.lindesmith.org/homepage.cfm
www.drugpolicy.org/homepage.cfm
www.cfdp.ca
www.camh.net
http://scotty-simmons.memory-of.com
www.freewebs.com/kennysims

Acknowledgements

I wish to acknowledge the support and continued enthusiasm of Altitude Publishing, who pepper me with great story ideas and encourage me to write for them.

I also wish to thank my girlfriend, Alyson Fischer, for her steadfast patience and love. I want to thank my parents for the same.

I want to extend an additional thanks to all the people I interviewed for this book, particularly the former meth users who were willing to be so open and upfront about their struggles with addiction. I wish them all well with their recoveries.

I am greatly indebted to Dr. Richard Rawson of Los Angeles' Matrix Institute. Dr. Rawson went beyond the call of duty in answering my interview questions and in sending me relevant literature on the topic of methamphetamine.

Doug Pamenter, of *www.crystalrecovery.*

com and Rashelle Chaplin, of *www.methmadness.com* were instrumental in steering me towards potential interview subjects. I also utilized a great amount of information posted at their web sites.

The folks at Crystal Meth Anonymous (CMA) were equally helpful in answering my questions and setting up interviews with their members.

Dave Parnell deserves a very special pat on the back as well. Parnell did not hesitate to provide deeply personal information about his sometimes violent battle with meth. He has made an astonishing recovery from a potentially deadly addiction. Parnell's story forms the centerpiece of this book.

Photo Credits

Identity Theft
by Rennay Craats

The scary new cri...
by Re...

*Plastic Surgery
Gone Wrong*

by Melanie
Jones

Tragic consequences in the search for beauty
by Melanie Jones